TROUT COOKBOOK

TROUT
COOKBOOK

60 CLASSIC RECIPES

JANE BAMFORTH

LORENZ BOOKS

This edition is published by Lorenz Books,
an imprint of Anness Publishing Ltd,
info@anness.com

www.lorenzbooks.com; www.annesspublishing.com;
twitter:@AnnessLorenzBks

© Anness Publishing Ltd 2018

Publisher: Joanna Lorenz
Jacket designer: Adelle Mahoney
Editorial: Helen Sudell
Recipes: Catherine Atkinson, Alex Barker, Jane Bamforth,
Ghillie Basan, Carla Capalbo, Jacqueline Clarke, Roz Denny,
Matthew Drennan, Joanna Farrow, Christine France, Brian
Glover, Becky Johnson, Christine Ingram, Liz Trigg, Linda
Tubby, Kate Whiteman, Elizabeth Wolf-Cohen, Deh-Ta
Hsuing, Terry Tan, Carol Wilson.
Photographers: Tim Auty, Martin Brigdale, Nicki Dowey,
James Duncan, Michelle Garrett, Amanda Heywood,
William Lingwood, Tom Odulate, Craig Robertson, William
Shaw, Sam Stowell.
Production controller: Ben Worley

PUBLISHER'S NOTE
Although the advice and information in this book are believed
to be accurate and true at the time of going to press, neither
the authors nor the publisher can accept any legal
responsibility or liability for any errors or omissions that may
have been made nor for any inaccuracies nor for any loss, harm
or injury that comes about from following instructions or advice
in this book.

COOK'S NOTES
Bracketed terms are intended for American readers.
For all recipes, quantities are given in both metric and
imperial measures and, where appropriate, in standard
cups and spoons. Follow one set of measures, but not a
mixture, because they are not interchangeable.
Standard spoon and cup measures are level.
1 tsp = 5ml, 1 tbsp = 15ml, 1 cup = 250ml/8fl oz.
Australian standard tablespoons are 20ml. Australian
readers should use 3 tsp in place of 1 tbsp for measuring
small quantities. American pints are 16fl oz/2 cups.
American readers should use 20fl oz/2.5 cups in place of
1 pint when measuring liquids.
Electric oven temperatures in this book are for
conventional ovens. When using a fan oven, the
temperature will probably need to be reduced by about
10–20°C/20–40°F. Since ovens vary, you should check
with your manufacturer's instruction book for guidance.
The nutritional analysis given for each recipe is calculated
per portion (i.e. serving or item), unless otherwise stated.
If the recipe gives a range, such as Serves 4–6, then the
nutritional analysis will be for the smaller portion size,
i.e. 6 servings. The analysis does not include optional
ingredients, such as salt added to taste.

Contents

INTRODUCTION

The best-known of all freshwater fish, trout is also one of the most popular. It is inexpensive to buy and readily available, which makes it the perfect ingredient for a variety of meals. Trout doesn't just taste fabulous, it has very high levels of omega-fatty acids, is low in fat and high in protein, so it is nutritionally good for you too.

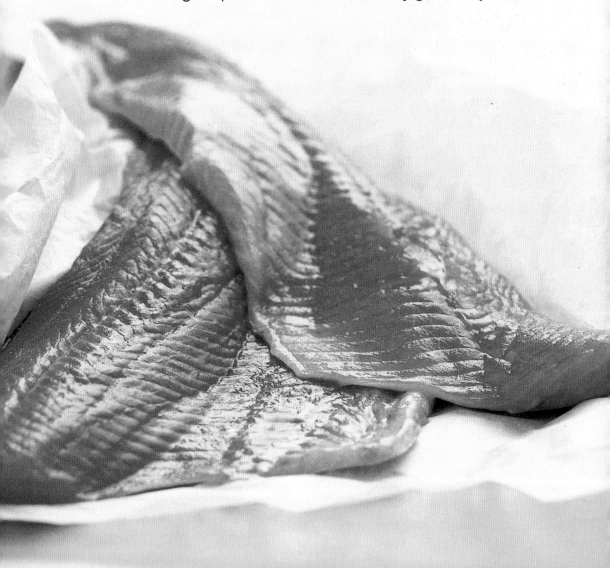

The story of trout

Above: Fly fishing on the Scottish border. This method of catching trout has been popular since ancient times.

Opposite: Freshly caught sea trout hung up ready for cooking over an open fire.

Ever since man first learned to catch trout, these fish have been invaluable as a source of food. Native Americans, ancient Britons and early Europeans all treasured these tasty fish, and it is no surprise that the fish hook was one of man's earliest tools.

Fishing rods were in use around four thousand years ago and it is known that the ancient Macedonians were adept at fly fishing for trout. They used the technique known as dapping, which involves dropping the artificial fly lightly on the surface of the water so that the fish thinks it is the real thing and takes the bait.

In a bid to increase the freshwater trout population, the ancient Chinese encouraged the fish to spawn on mats placed in rivers. The mats were then lifted out and the fertilized eggs were used to stock new breeding sites. The first person to artificially fertilize trout eggs is said to have been a French monk. The eggs were tightly packed in wooden boxes and buried in sand underground until they hatched.

RANGE AND HABITAT

Like salmon, to which they are related, trout are native to the northern hemisphere, but they are also highly successful emigrants. Brown trout are native to Europe but they thrive in America. Conversely, the American rainbow trout has been successfully introduced to many other parts of the world. In New Zealand, for instance, the rainbow trout has acclimatized so successfully that many inhabitants of that country believe it to be one of their own native species.

LIFE CYCLE

There are many similarities between trout and salmon and both spawn in gravel pits, or redds, in fresh water. The young trout hatch after about 30 days. Initially they remain hidden in the gravel, feeding off their yolk sacs, but when this supply of food is exhausted they emerge. At this stage they are known as fry. As they grow, they develop markings, like fingerprints, on the sides of their bodies, and are described as parr, the name deriving from an Old English word for finger. Like young salmon, trout remain in their home waters for an initial period before swimming further afield to feed. Unlike salmon,

Above: Sea trout on sale at a local fish market. Try to cook it on the day of purchase.

however, most trout are fairly modest in their aspirations, moving to a larger river or lake rather than the ocean, although some species have adapted to living in salt water as well as fresh. Sea trout, cutthroat trout and steelhead rainbow trout are in this category. When they are several years old, the skins of these anadromous (i.e. migratory) fish become silvery and they are then known as smolts. They spend most of their lives at sea, only returning to fresh water to spawn.

When and where individual species spawn depends on the variety of trout, the water temperature and other local conditions. Trout eggs hatch earlier than those of salmon, giving the fry time to establish themselves before their larger relatives appear on the scene.

There is considerable size variation between trout of different species and within the species themselves. The average rainbow trout on sale at the fishmongers weighs around 350g/12oz but fishermen have reported catching fish in excess of 12kg/26lb. Sea trout that evade capture can survive for many years and grow to over 40kg/88lb, although most fish sold commercially weigh about 3kg/6½lb.

FARMING TROUT

Trout have been raised in captivity since the 1850s, initially with the aim of re-stocking freshwater rivers and lakes, but more recently for supply to the consumer. In the early years of the 20th century, a Danish trout farmer developed a system for introducing a flow of fresh water into his fish ponds to imitate river conditions. This helped reduce disease and led to improved yields.

The first commercial fish farm in England was opened in 1950 and there are now more than 300 farms in the United Kingdom alone. Most farmed trout in the United States comes from Idaho and is considered one of the healthiest fish to eat by the Monterey Bay Aquarium's Seafood Watch. As with salmon, it is very important to buy farmed trout from a responsible producer who cares for the environment as well as for his or her fish. Some agrochemical farmers pollute rivers with pesticides, waste fish food and sewage. The trout are packed into pens, and this makes them vulnerable to disease and infestation by fish lice.

In the wild, trout flesh is often pale pink, due to its natural diet. Some producers of farmed fish add colorants to the feed to mimic this. Organically farmed trout have creamy white flesh.

NUTRITION
Naturally low in sodium, fat, cholesterol and calories, trout is a highly nutritious food, especially if it is steamed, grilled or cooked in the microwave. It is high in omega-3 fatty acids, which lower blood triglycerides and reduce blood pressure, protecting the body against coronary and cardiovascular disease. Trout is also a useful source of vitamins A, B1, B2, C and D. A 100g/ 3½oz portion of grilled rainbow trout delivers 631kj/151kcals.

COOKING
Frying freshly caught trout over an open fire on the river bank may be the ideal, but there are many other ways of cooking this delicious fish, including poaching in court-bouillon, baking, braising, grilling, broiling, and cooking on a barbecue. Whole trout is easy to eat, as the cooked flesh falls away from the bone, but it can also be flaked and added to salads, rice or pasta dishes.

Above: Barbecuing trout takes just a few minutes and is a delicious addition to any alfresco meal.

Left: Grilling trout over an open fire is still the classic way of cooking this wonderful fish.

Types of trout

Above: Sea trout.

There are several different types of trout. Like salmon, they all originated in the northern hemisphere, but are now widely distributed. Although some people declare that brown trout tastes better than rainbow trout, the reality is that all types are very similar in flavour, and any variations are determined more by diet and location than variety. The texture of good quality trout is fine and firm.

Most wild trout eat a selection of plankton and small crustaceans, which gives their flesh a beautiful rose colour. In Australia, trout that feed on yabbies are particularly highly prized. Some trout farmers use carotene-rich feed so that their fish develop flesh of a similar colour to that of trout in the wild, but others, especially those who farm organically, avoid this and produce fish with creamy-coloured flesh.

BROWN TROUT (Salmo trutta)
Also known as river or lake trout, brown trout are native to Europe, but are now widely distributed throughout the world. In appearance, brown trout vary considerably. Even in the same stretch of water, some will be a silver colour, while others will be almost black. The typical colour is brown with a red adipose (rear top) fin, yellow belly, bright red spots and a liberal sprinkling of black speckles. The more silver forms can be mistaken for rainbow trout. The flesh is very tasty, with a slightly earthy flavour. The brown trout's freshwater diet includes invertebrates from the streambed, other fish, frogs, birds and insects flying near the water's surface. Feeding so close to the water's surface makes them a favoured target for fly fishing.

SEA TROUT (Salmo trutta)
Sharp-eyed readers will have noticed that this trout has the same Latin name as brown trout. That's because scientists believe them to be the same fish, despite the differences in size and behaviour. At one time it was thought that sea trout were a separate species, because they are anadromous, like salmon, and spend most of their lives at sea, but it is now thought that they are merely a migratory form of brown trout. Sea trout are always wild, but they do not cost as much as wild salmon. They are sold whole and should be bright and

silvery in colour with an almost golden sheen. The fish for sale in fishmongers and supermarkets typically weigh between 2kg/4½lb and 3kg/6½lb, with one fish enough to serve 4–6 people. Sea trout have fine, succulent, dark pink flesh and a delicate, rounded flavour.

Above: Brown (right) and rainbow trout.

RAINBOW TROUT (Oncorhynchus mykiss)
Native to North America, this highly successful fish is now found in lakes and streams in Australia, New Zealand, Central and South America, and South Africa. It is the most popular breed for fish farming. It has tender flesh and a mild, somewhat nutty flavour. The base colour of the body is a creamy white colour, with an iridescent sheen. There is a dense black spotting on the back and sides. Many anglers consider the rainbow trout the hardest of the trout species to catch.

Above: The California golden trout, or simply the golden trout, is a subspecies of the rainbow trout native to California.

Opposite: Smaller trout can be smoked whole.

CUTTHROAT TROUT (Oncorhynchus clarkii)

Taking its popular name from the yellow, orange or red slash marks on either side of the lower jaw, this fish has a similar distribution to the rainbow trout, but unlike rainbow trout, most cutthroats migrate to sea when they are fully mature. They have tasty, tender flesh, which ranges from a cream colour to deep red, depending on the local diet.

GOLDEN TROUT (Oncorhynchus mykiss aguabonita)

This is the state fish of California. Golden trout, like coral trout, is a farmed hybrid variety, with vibrant skin and delicious red flesh that is firmer than that of its close relation, the rainbow trout. The bright colouring makes both types of trout vulnerable to predators, but as farmed fish they are almost always bred and raised in a protected environment.

SMOKED TROUT

Once dismissed as poor man's smoked salmon, smoked trout is now regarded as a delicious treat in its own right. To prepare it, the fish are first brined, then cured in salt and sugar before being cold or hot smoked over oak or birch chippings. The colour ranges from rose pink to reddish brown and the best smoked trout is beautifully moist, with a more delicate flavour than that of smoked herring or mackerel. Smoked trout is usually sold as skinned fillets, but you will occasionally find them whole.

Smoked trout has a wonderful flavour and tastes delicious when served simply with bread and butter. Horseradish cream and capers are often served as accompaniments. The fish also makes a very good pâté, or can be added to omelettes, risottos, quiches or pasta dishes. Allow one fillet per person as an appetizer; two as a main course.

TROUT ROE

Translucent orange beads of trout roe make a glorious garnish for savoury dishes. It can also be eaten in the same way as caviar, with sour cream and blinis for a delicious hors d'oeuvre to accompany a chilled glass of wine. Try the roe spread on fingers of wholemeal or whole-wheat toast, or spooned over crème fraîche in tiny pastry cases.

Buying and preparing trout

Above: When buying fresh trout look for bright, shiny eyes, and a cold but firm skin that is slimy to the touch.

Wild trout is difficult to come by, unless you happen to enjoy fly fishing. Most of the trout on sale in fish shops and supermarkets is farmed, and is likely to be rainbow trout or one of its hybrids. Brown trout is available from some specialist suppliers, and it is always worth trawling the Internet for details of organic fish farmers who will deliver your order. Make sure that the fish will be delivered within 24 hours, in an insulated container, and place a small order in the first instance so that you can satisfy yourself as to the quality of the fish and its condition on receipt. Frozen trout is also a good buy and the fish is usually in prime condition.

Sea trout is not farmed, and you will almost certainly need to order it from your fishmonger or market. This large fish has an excellent flavour and is often substituted for the more expensive salmon. Sea trout is always sold whole.

When buying fresh trout in person, the same rules apply as for any other fresh fish. Look for fish that have shiny, iridescent skins, with a good coating of slime, bright clear eyes and red gills. The skin should feel cold to the touch, and when pressed, should spring back instantly. If any indentation remains, the fish is not as fresh as it might be. Trout are almost always sold whole with the head on, which you can use to make fish stock with if you prefer not to cook it.

Unless they are particularly large, you should allow one trout per person if you plan to serve it whole. A 2kg/4½lb sea trout will be sufficient to serve 4–6 people. If cooking trout fillets as part of a recipe, follow the quantity given in the instructions.

When buying fresh trout, transport it in a chiller bag. Double wrap it when you get home and store it in the coldest part of the refrigerator. Aim to cook it on the same day. If this is not possible, store it for no more than two days, or freeze it. Trout freezes very well. Thaw it slowly, overnight in the refrigerator if possible.

PREPARATION
If you buy trout from a fishmonger or supermarket, it will have been cleaned, but you might be lucky enough to be offered some freshly caught trout on some occasion. In this case it is essential to know how to prepare it.

Trout do not need to be scaled, but it is a good idea to remove the fins as these can harbour bacteria. Cut them off using a strong pair of scissors. Take care with the dorsal fins (those on the back), which can have sharp spines.

CLEANING TROUT

This can be performed quickly and easily with preparation. Start by spreading the work area with newspapers and topping these with greaseproof or waxed paper.

There are two ways of gutting whole trout: through the belly or through the gills. The former is the more usual method, but gutting through the gills is preferred if splitting the fish open would spoil its appearance. In either case, the gills should be removed before the fish is cooked, because they taste bitter. Do this by holding the fish on its back and opening the gill flaps. Push out the frilly gills and cut them off at the back of the head and under the jawbone.

Cleaning through the belly: This is the usual way of cleaning trout. Assemble your equipment and cover the work surface before you begin.
1 Starting at the site of the anal fin, slit open the belly from tail to head, using a sharp filleting knife (top right).
2 Pull out the innards, severing them at the throat and tail if necessary (top middle right). If you are planning to stuff the trout, the roes will make a delicious addition.
3 Use a tablespoon to make sure the cavity is empty, removing any blood vessels adjacent to the backbone. Double wrap the innards and throw them away in an outside bin. Wash the cavity, then pat dry with kitchen paper.

Cleaning through the gills: If you are planning to serve the trout whole, it is better to clean through the gills to preserve its appearance.
1 Lay the fish on its side. Make an incision in the belly near the tail (bottom middle right). Find the ends of the innards and snip through.
2 Cut through the bone under the lower jaw. Open the gill flaps and pull out the innards (bottom right); they will come away through the flaps. Wash and dry the fish.

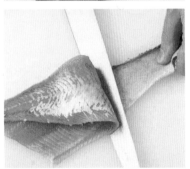

Filleting trout: This is a useful technique to learn if you want to cut fillets from a whole trout.

1 Lay the trout on a board with its tail towards you. Lift the pectoral fin and make a diagonal cut behind the fin to the top of the head (top left).

2 Insert the knife halfway down the body, as close to the backbone as possible. Cut towards the tail, keeping the knife flat to the bone. Lift up the released fillet, turn the knife towards the head and slide it along the bone to free the fillet completely (top middle left).

3 Turn the trout over and repeat the other side. Remove any small pin bones from the fillets with tweezers (see Cook's Tip). Skin the fillets if you like.

Skinning trout fillets: If the recipe requires the skin to be taken off the fillets it is a simple procedure.

1 Lay the fillet skin side down with the tail towards you. Grip the tail and angle the knife towards the skin.

2 With a slight sawing action, cut along the length of the fillet from tail to head (bottom middle left). Keep the skin taut.

Boning a trout steak: If you are serving trout steaks to children you may wish to take out the central bone before grilling the steaks.

1 Insert a sharp, thin-bladed knife into the trout cutlet at the top of the bone. Cut around the bone until you reach the centre of the V-shape of the cutlet.

2 Repeat on the other side of the steak, to free the bone completely. Gently pull out the bone (bottom left). Skin the fish if you want to make it more manageable.

3 Fold the skinned flesh in the middle and tie with a length of string to hold the shape.

COOK'S TIP There are always some small bones left in a fillet. Run your finger down the fillet to locate these and lift them out with a pair of tweezers.

Round fish also have tiny pin bones behind the gill fins. To remove these, make a diagonal cut on either side of the line of bones with a sharp knife. Using tweezers, remove the V-shaped piece of flesh together with the bones.

Cooking trout

The secret of cooking trout successfully is the same as that for any other type of fish: less time means more taste. Undercooking can easily be remedied, but fish that is overcooked is dry and flavourless. Although the very best way to cook a fresh wild brown trout is to fry it in butter, farmed rainbow trout can be cooked in a variety of ways.

Trout is available all year round from many supermarkets, individual shops, local fishmongers or direct from fish-farm shops. It can be also purchased online fresh or frozen, as fillets, steaks or whole fish and also comes in hot and cold smoked varieties.

POACHING
For a whole trout, you will need a fish kettle, flameproof dish or roasting pan; for smaller cuts, use an ordinary pan.
1 Remove the metal insert from the fish kettle and place the trout on this. Lower into the kettle. Add a few sprigs of fresh herbs and slices of lemon (top right).

2 Pour cold court-bouillon, light fish stock or water over the trout in the fish kettle, adding enough of the liquid to cover the fish completely.
3 Cover the trout with buttered baking parchment (top middle right). Bring the liquid slowly to simmering point. If poaching fillets, thin portions may now be cooked and can be removed. Lower the heat, cover the pan and poach the uncooked thicker fillets for 5 minutes more or until done.

Court-bouillon: This classic stock, which is lightly flavoured with white wine and aromatics, is perfect for poaching trout. Any salt should be added only after cooking, as it can cause the flesh to stiffen. The recipe makes approximately 1 litre/ 1¾ pints/4 cups.
1 Slice 1 small onion, 2 carrots and the white part of 1 large leek (bottom middle right). Put the vegetables in a pan.

2 Add 2 fresh parsley stalks, 2 bay leaves, 2 lemon slices 300ml/½ pint/1¼ cups dry white wine and 90ml/6 tbsp white wine vinegar (bottom right). Sprinkle in a few white peppercorns. Pour in 1 litre/1¾ pints/4 cups water. Bring to the boil, lower the heat and simmer for 20 minutes. Strain and leave to cool before using.

Fish stock: A stock made from fish bones, heads and other trimmings is the backbone of bouillabaisse, chowder, paella, and other classic dishes. It is both easy and economical to make. For 1 litre/1¾ pints/4 cups stock you will need about 1kg/2¼lb white fish bones and trimmings from the fishmonger. Do not leave the stock simmering for too long – after 20 minutes the flavour will start to deteriorate.

1 Wash any fish heads thoroughly and remove the gills, which would make the stock bitter. Chop the heads and bones if necessary. Put them in a large pan (top left).

2 Slice the white part of 1 leek or ½ fennel bulb. Roughly chop 1 onion and 1 celery stick. Add to the fish heads and bones in the pan.

3 Pour in 150ml/¼ pint/⅔ cup dry white wine and 1 litre/1¾ pints/4 cups water. Add 6 whole white peppercorns and a bouquet garni (middle left). Bring to the boil. Lower the heat and simmer for 20 minutes. Remove from the heat, strain through a sieve lined with muslin (cheesecloth) and cool.

COOKING 'AU BLEU'

This time-honoured way of cooking trout is only for the freshest fish – so fresh that it is alive seconds before you begin the process. The term 'au bleu' refers to the steely blue colour the fish skin acquires on being poached.

To cook trout 'au bleu' the live fish is taken from the water and immediately stunned by a hit on the back of the head with a blunt object, such as the handle of a heavy cook's knife or a steak mallet. The fish is then cleaned through the gills and laid in a flameproof dish or fish kettle. A mixture of water and white wine vinegar is spooned over to cover it completely (bottom left), and the fish is then gently simmered over a medium heat until it is cooked.

A 150g/5oz trout will take 6–8 minutes, during which time the natural slime that coats the very fresh fish will turn a deep blue colour – from which the cooking method takes its name. Trout prepared in this way is traditionally served hot with hollandaise sauce, or cold with Ravigote sauce – made by mixing oil and vinegar with chopped tomatoes, diced hard-boiled eggs, capers, chopped gherkins and fresh parsley, tarragon and chervil.

BAKING

Whole trout, steaks or fillets can all be baked in the oven. It is an excellent way of cooking trout slowly, along with extra flavourings, such as fresh herbs, or vegetables. Slash whole fish to allow the heat to penetrate the flesh.

1 Lay the fish in a greased baking dish, drizzle with olive oil and add a little liquid (top right). Dry (hard) cider goes well with trout, as do court-bouillon and fish stock. Cover with buttered baking parchment or foil and bake at no more than 200°C/ 400°F/Gas 6. Whole fish will cook in 20–30 minutes, depending on the thickness. Trout fillets will cook more quickly. It is important not to overcook them.

En papillote: To seal in the flavour and retain moisture, bake the trout en papillote in a paper or foil parcel. A stuffing of rice with nuts and sun-dried tomatoes would be an excellent addition. Place the trout on a piece of oiled baking parchment or foil and fill the cavity with the stuffing. Add a drizzle of olive oil. Add a few herbs and a slice of lemon and fold over the paper or foil to enclose the fish completely (middle right). Place the parcel on a baking sheet. Bake at 190°C/375°F/ Gas 5 for about 20 minutes, until the trout is tender and the flesh falls away easily from the bones.

BRAISING

This is an ideal way of cooking either whole trout or fillets and takes no time at all to produce a melt-in-the-mouth dish. Adding the stock helps to keep the fish beautifully moist and the vegetables in the braising liquid double up as a side dish.

1 Butter a flameproof dish and arrange a thick bed of thinly sliced or shredded vegetables on the base, such as a mixture of leeks, fennel and carrots.

2 Place the fish on top of the vegetables and pour on enough dry white wine, court-bouillon or light fish stock to come nearly halfway up the fish.

3 Scatter over 15ml/1 tbsp chopped fresh herbs, then cover with buttered baking parchment (bottom right) and set over a high heat. Bring the liquid to the boil. Braise over a low heat on top of the stove or in an oven preheated to 180°C/350°F/ Gas 4 for 10–15 minutes.

FRYING

Pan-frying is a fabulously tasty way to cook trout, but stir-frying in a wok uses less oil and is a healthier alternative.

Pan-frying: Boned whole trout, steaks and fillets can be pan-fried in butter. Butter burns quite readily; adding a little oil will help prevent this. Coat the fish in seasoned flour before adding it to the melted butter, and fry over a low heat. If using whole trout, cook for 6 minutes on each side, until the skin is crisp and golden brown.

Searing: Smear a frying pan with a little oil and heat until smoking. Brush both sides of the fish with oil and put into the pan skin-side down. Sear for 2 minutes until the skin is golden brown (top left), turn the fish over, and cook on the other side.

Stir-frying: Strips of trout fillet can be stir-fried in a hot wok for 1–2 minutes, but take care that they do not disintegrate (middle left). Toss the fish strips with a little sweet chilli sauce just before serving.

Deep-frying: Trout pieces are transformed into goujons by coating them in milk and flour and deep-frying in oil. Dip strips of trout fillet into milk, and then into a plate of plain (all-purpose) flour that has been seasoned with salt and ground black pepper. Shake off the excess flour. Heat oil for deep-frying to about 180°C/360°F or until a small cube of bread dropped into the oil turns brown in 30 seconds. Lower the trout strips into the oil and fry for 3 minutes, turning with a slotted spoon, until they rise to the surface. Drain the goujons on kitchen paper (bottom left) and serve.

GRILLING

This is one of the best ways of cooking farmed rainbow trout. If grilling or broiling the trout whole, slash the skin on either side of the fish several times with a sharp knife. This helps to promote fast, even cooking. Marinate whole trout or steaks in a mixture of oil and lemon juice if you like, or simply brush with oil. Place the trout in a grill pan and cook under a medium heat for 5 minutes on each side.

MICROWAVING

Cover the fish with microwave clear film or plastic wrap and cook on full power (100 per cent) for the time recommended in your handbook, then give it a resting period so that it finishes cooking by residual heat. As a general guide, a whole fish will take 4–7 minutes, depending on whether or not it has been stuffed. Leave to stand for a further 5 minutes before serving. Slash whole fish several times on either side for even cooking. Cook fillets of trout in a single layer in a microwave dish. Put thinner parts towards the centre, or tuck a thin end underneath a thicker portion (top right).

STEAMING

As no extra fat is required and all of the nutrients are retained, this is the healthiest way to cook trout.
1 Half-fill the base pan of a steamer with water and bring to the boil. Place the trout fillets in a single layer in the steamer basket, leaving room for the steam to circulate (middle right).
2 Place a sheet of baking parchment over the fish, then cover the pan and steam until the fish is cooked through. Check the level of water in the steamer.

SMOKING

Trout can be smoked at home, either in a small domestic smoker or a kettle barbecue. Follow the instructions in your handbook. In the kitchen, the Chinese method of tea smoking works very well.
1 Line a wok with foil and sprinkle in 30ml/2 tbsp each of raw long grain rice, sugar and aromatic tea leaves.
2 Place a wire rack on the wok and add the trout fillets in a single layer. Cover with a lid or more foil and cook over a high heat until smoke appears (bottom right). Lower the heat slightly (some smoke should still escape from the wok) and cook for 6–8 minutes until the trout is done.

COOK'S TIP If you do not own a steamer, a good way to cook trout fillets over water is to place them in a single layer on a buttered heatproof plate. Cover this with an inverted heatproof plate of the same size, lift both plates together and place them over a pan of boiling water. The fillets will cook in 3–4 minutes.

BARBECUING

The oil in trout makes it a good candidate for barbecue cooking. If using thawed frozen trout, pat it dry inside and out with kitchen paper. Brush with oil and sprinkle with salt and ground black pepper. The fish can be cooked directly on a lightly oiled grill, although you may find it easier to turn them over if the fish are placed in a hinged grilling rack. For a deeper flavour, marinate the trout in a mixture of olive oil and lemon juice, making deep slashes in the sides of the fish so that the marinade penetrates right the way through and the heat is conducted evenly. Allow the fish to marinate in the refrigerator for a minimum of 1 hour.

Whole trout are also wonderful filled with flavourings. Try lemon and lime slices combined with one or more of the following – sprigs of parsley, dill or fennel, or bay leaves – packed inside the cleaned fish, as these flavourings will complement the delicate taste of the fish without overpowering it. Once filled, the fish can be wrapped in foil before barbecuing. If you do this, you could add more flavourings inside the packet.

Cook over medium-hot coals for about 10–15 minutes, or until done, and turn once, halfway through cooking. Drizzle with fresh lemon juice just before serving.

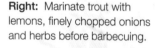

Right: Marinate trout with lemons, finely chopped onions and herbs before barbecuing.

Essential equipment

Although it is perfectly possible to prepare and cook fish without special kitchen equipment, there are a few items which make the process much easier.

Chef's knife: A large heavy knife with a 20–25cm/8–10in blade is essential for cutting fish steaks.

Filleting knife: For filleting and skinning fish, you will need a sharp knife with a flexible blade, which is at least 15cm/6in long. This type of knife can also be used for opening shellfish.

Kitchen scissors: A sturdy pair of scissors with a serrated edge are needed for cutting off fins and trimming tails.

Fish scaler: Resembling a small grater, a fish scaler makes short work of a task that few relish.

Fish kettle: Long and deep, with rounded edges, this has handles at either end, and a tightly-fitting lid (top right). Inside is a perforated rack or grid on which to lay the fish. This, too, has handles, and enables the cook to lift out the fish flat, without breaking it. Most modern fish kettles are made of stainless steel, but they also come in aluminium, enamelled steel and copper with a tin-plated interior. Fish kettles are used on the hob and are invaluable for cooking whole large fish. Fish kettles can also be used for steaming other foods.

Barbecue grilling rack: A hinged rack in the shape of a fish makes cooking – and turning – a single large fish relatively easy (middle right). Always oil grilling racks before use to prevent the fish from sticking to them.

Fish smoker: The cheapest home-smoker is a lidded metal box with a rack to hold the fish. Smoke produced by placing dampened aromatic oak or other wood chippings, or a scattering of fresh herbs, on the coals gives extra flavour to the fish. More convenient (but more expensive) are electric fish smokers. Stove-top models can be used indoors.

Fish lifter: Resembling an elongated fish slice, the curved and perforated turner is useful for flipping over whole trout during cooking without breaking them.

Fish slice: A fish slice will make easy work of turning whole trout, steaks and cutlets (bottom right).

Tweezers: Use these to extract small bones and pin bones from fish fillets.

APPETIZERS AND LIGHT BITES

One of the many attributes of trout is its delicate pink colour. Trout Bisque looks so delicious in the bowl that it would seem a shame to disturb it, were it not for the wonderful aroma that rises from the surface. Salads, tarts, toasties and mousses are just as pretty, especially when smoked trout is used as a wrapper, as in Three Fish Mousse.

Trout bisque

SERVES 4

15ml/1 tbsp olive oil

1 onion, chopped

1 red (bell) pepper, finely chopped

1 garlic clove, crushed

1 medium potato, diced

2 tomatoes, skinned and chopped (see Cook's Tip)

300ml/½ pint/1¼ cups fish stock

225g/8oz trout fillet, skinned and diced

1.5ml/¼ tsp chilli powder

15ml/1 tbsp chopped fresh tarragon

300ml/½ pint/1¼ cups milk

30ml/2 tbsp dry sherry

150ml/¼ pint/⅔ cup double (heavy) cream

salt and ground black pepper

sprigs of watercress, to garnish

A bisque is a thick, rich, smooth soup, usually containing fish or shellfish. This wonderfully coloured pale pink version has a deliciously creamy texture with a hint of spiciness. Serve it with crusty bread and some unsalted butter.

1 Heat the olive oil in a large pan, and add the onion, pepper, garlic and potato. Fry gently for 5 minutes, stirring constantly, until the onion has just softened.

2 Add the tomatoes and stock to the pan, increase the heat and bring to the boil. Then reduce the heat and allow to simmer for 10 minutes or until the vegetables are soft.

3 Add the trout, chilli powder and chopped tarragon. Simmer gently for a further 5 minutes or until the fish is just cooked and is starting to flake when tested with a fork.

4 Remove the pan from the heat, and stir in half the milk. Set aside for 20–30 minutes to allow the contents to cool.

5 Pour the fish and vegetable mixture into a food processor and blend until smooth. Scrape into a clean pan and stir in the sherry and cream, with the remaining milk.

6 Heat the soup gently, stirring, until piping hot. Season to taste, then divide among soup bowls, garnish and serve.

COOK'S TIP To skin the tomatoes, cut a small cross on the base of each tomato. Pour boiling water over and leave for 1 minute. The skin will then peel off very easily.

Smoked trout cocottes

Hot smoked trout fillets taste quite different from cold smoked trout; they have a surprisingly creamy texture and a wonderful pale pink colour. This dish makes a perfect light lunch for two people, or a first course for four.

1 Preheat the oven to 180°C/350°F/Gas 4. Place the peppers in a roasting pan. Drizzle with olive oil and season well with salt and pepper. Bake for 25–30 minutes or until the pepper skins are blackened. Set aside to cool.

2 Peel the skin off the cooked peppers and discard the core and seeds. Cut the pepper flesh into bitesize pieces.

3 Preheat the oven to 200°C/400°F/Gas 6. Flake the trout and divide between individual baking dishes. Arrange the pepper pieces in a layer over the fish in each dish.

4 Sprinkle the parsley over the fish and peppers. Spoon the crème fraîche into the dishes and season well. Top with the grated Parmesan cheese.

5 Bake in the preheated oven for about 15 minutes, or until the Parmesan cheese is golden brown and bubbling. Serve with chunks of sun-dried tomato bread, if you like.

COOK'S TIP If making this dish for a supper party first course, you can prepare it in advance, if you like. Keep it in the refrigerator and bake just before serving.

SERVES 2-4

4 red (bell) peppers

60ml/4 tbsp olive oil

150g/5oz hot smoked trout fillets

30ml/2 tbsp chopped fresh parsley

175g/6oz/¾ cup crème fraîche

50g/2oz Parmesan cheese, grated

salt and ground black pepper

sun-dried tomato bread, to serve

Sea trout mousse

SERVES 6

250g/9oz sea trout fillet

120ml/4fl oz/½ cup fish stock

2 sheets leaf gelatine, or 15ml/1 tbsp powdered gelatine

juice of ½ lemon

30ml/2 tbsp dry sherry or dry vermouth

30ml/2 tbsp freshly grated Parmesan cheese

300ml/½ pint/1¼ cups whipping cream

2 egg whites

15ml/1 tbsp sunflower oil

salt and ground white pepper

5cm/2in piece cucumber, with peel, halved and thinly sliced and fresh dill or chervil, to garnish

This deliciously creamy mousse makes a little sea trout go a long way. If you can't locate sea trout, it is equally good with rainbow trout.

1 Put the sea trout in a shallow pan. Pour in the fish stock and heat to simmering point. Poach the fish for about 3–4 minutes, until it is lightly cooked. Strain the stock into a jug or pitcher and leave the fish to cool.

2 Add the gelatine to the hot stock and stir until it has dissolved completely. Set the stock aside until required.

3 When the trout is cool enough to handle, remove the skin and flake the flesh. Pour the stock into a food processor or blender. Process briefly, then gradually add the flaked trout, lemon juice, sherry or vermouth and Parmesan through the feeder tube, continuing to process the mixture until it is smooth. Scrape into a bowl and leave to cool completely.

4 Lightly whip the cream in a bowl; fold it into the cold trout mixture. Season to taste, then cover with clear film (plastic wrap) and chill until the mousse is just beginning to set. It should have the consistency of mayonnaise.

5 In a grease-free bowl, beat the egg whites with a pinch of salt until they form soft peaks. Using a large metal spoon, stir one-third into the trout mixture to slacken it, then fold in the rest.

6 Lightly grease six ramekins with the sunflower oil. Divide the mousse among the ramekins and level the surface. Chill in the refrigerator for 2–3 hours, until set. Just before serving, arrange a few slices of cucumber and a small herb sprig on each mousse and add a little chopped dill or chervil.

COOK'S TIP Serve the mousse with Melba toast. Toast thin slices of bread on both sides under the grill or broiler. Cut off the crusts and slice each piece of toast in half. Return to the grill pan, untoasted sides up, and toast again, taking care not to let it burn.

Trout and prawn pots

Bacon is often wrapped around whole trout to keep the flesh moist when grilling, but here it has another function, to marry the flavours of trout and prawn. These pots can be made in advance and baked just before serving. Store the prepared pots in the refrigerator until you are ready to cook.

1 Heat the butter and oil in a heavy frying pan and fry the leek gently for 5 minutes or until softened, stirring occasionally.

2 Add the bacon to the pan and fry until it is just beginning to turn colour, stirring all the time. Add the prawns, increase the heat and stir-fry for 5 minutes. Remove from the heat.

3 Cut the trout fillet into bitesize pieces and stir into the bacon and prawn mixture. Season with a little salt, if required, and plenty of pepper. Divide the mixture among six ramekins.

4 Preheat the oven to 190°C/375°F/Gas 5. In a jug or pitcher beat the sour cream and egg with a fork. Season lightly. Pour one-sixth of the mixture into each ramekin and sprinkle the grated cheese over the top.

5 Bake the pots in the preheated oven for 15 minutes or until the top is golden brown and bubbling. Serve straight from the oven with chunks of warm, crusty bread, if you like.

SERVES 6

15g/½oz/1 tbsp butter

15ml/1 tbsp olive oil

1 small leek, finely chopped

2 rashers (strips) rindless back (lean) bacon, chopped

115g/4oz cooked peeled prawns (shrimp)

115g/4oz trout fillet, skinned

150ml/¼ pint/²/₃ cup sour cream

1 egg, beaten

50g/2oz Cheddar cheese, grated

salt and ground black pepper

warm country bread, to serve

Three fish mousse

SERVES 6-8

15ml/1 tbsp oil
450g/1lb cod fillet, skinned
1 bay leaf
1 slice lemon
6 black peppercorns
275g/10oz thinly sliced smoked trout
60ml/4 tbsp cold water
15g/½oz powdered gelatine
175g/6oz cooked peeled prawns (shrimp), halved
300ml/½ pint/1¼ cups sour cream
225g/8oz/1 cup cream cheese
30ml/2 tbsp chopped fresh dill
juice of 1 lemon
3 drops Tabasco sauce
salt and ground black pepper
sprigs of fresh herbs, such as parsley or dill, and 6–8 lemon wedges, to garnish

A rich and creamy mousse which is flavoured with lemon and dill – two of the classic partners for a wide range of fish and shellfish. This would make a stunning first course, or it could be served with crusty bread for a tasty lunch.

1 Lightly oil a 1.2 litre/2 pint/5 cup ring mould. Place the cod, bay leaf, lemon and peppercorns in a pan. Cover with cold water and bring to simmering point. Poach for 10–15 minutes, or until the fish flakes when tested with a fork.

2 Meanwhile, line the oiled ring mould with overlapping slices of smoked trout, leaving plenty hanging over the edge.

3 Remove the cod from the pan with a fish slice or metal spatula. Reserve the stock to use for another recipe. Chop the cod into bitesize chunks and put it in a large bowl.

4 Place the measured cold water in a heatproof bowl and sprinkle the gelatine over the surface. Leave for 5 minutes, until spongy, then place the bowl over a pan of hot water. Stir until the gelatine has dissolved. Leave to cool slightly.

5 Add the prawns, sour cream, cream cheese and dill to the cod in the bowl. Pour in the lemon juice and Tabasco sauce. Using a fork, mash the mixture together until well combined. Season to taste with salt and plenty of ground black pepper.

6 Using a large metal spoon, fold the dissolved gelatine into the fish mixture, making sure it is evenly incorporated. Spoon into the lined ring mould and smooth down the top.

7 Lift the overhanging edges of the smoked trout and fold them over the top of the mousse. Cover the mousse with clear film or plastic wrap and chill in the refrigerator for at least 2 hours or until set.

8 To serve, carefully run a round-bladed knife around the edge of the mousse, invert a serving plate on top and turn both over. Shake mould and plate together, if necessary, until the mousse drops out on to the plate. Garnish with the herbs and lemon wedges and serve.

Smoked trout terrine

This beautifully textured terrine is very simple to make but looks fabulous – perfect to impress dinner guests, or to be the star attraction at an alfresco lunch. Serve with toasted bread and thin slices of tomato.

1 Cook the carrot in a pan of boiling water for 10 minutes, until softened. Drain and refresh under cold running water. Line a non-stick, 6cm/2½in-deep rectangular cake tin or pan with the slices of carrot.

2 Place the gelatine in a small bowl of cold water and leave to soak for 5 minutes, until softened. Meanwhile, bring the cream just to the boil in a small pan, then remove from the heat. Squeeze out the gelatine and dissolve it in the cream. Stir in the dill and season generously with salt and pepper.

3 Pour a layer of cream into the cake tin, place a trout fillet on top and cover with another layer of cream. Continue making layers until all the cream and fish have been used up. Chill the terrine in the refrigerator for 8 hours or overnight.

4 About 30 minutes before you are ready to serve, turn out the terrine and cut it into slices. Arrange the slices on a serving plate and leave to come to room temperature. Garnish with lettuce and tomato slices and serve with toast.

MAKES 9 SLICES

1 large carrot, thinly sliced

15g/½oz gelatine leaves

500ml/17fl oz/generous 2 cups double (heavy) cream

30ml/2 tbsp finely chopped fresh dill

5 smoked trout fillets

salt and ground white pepper

oakleaf or frisée lettuce, toasted white bread and tomato slices, to serve

Tea-smoked trout

If you have access to a fish smoker it can be fun to smoke your own fish. In this classic South African dish the trout is first cured to remove excess moisture before it is smoked with a little rooibos tea. For an unusual twist the fish is served with lime pickle on the side.

1 To cure the fish, combine the salt, sugar, coriander, allspice berries, chilli flakes and chopped dill in a small bowl. Sprinkle this mixture on to a medium baking tray or a large dinner plate.

2 Place the fish fillets, skin-side up, on to the salt and sugar mixture. Press the flesh side into the cure mix, then turn over so the fillets are skin-side down. Leave for 2–3 hours in the refrigerator. When the fish has had its cure, wash off the mixture under cold running water. Pat dry with kitchen paper.

3 Cut out a circle of foil about 10cm/4½in in diameter, then fashion it into a shallow bowl shape. Place in the bottom of a smoking box, potjie, or casserole pan and fill it with the tea leaves.

4 Place a small bowl beside the foil bowl and fill this with ice. Place the fish fillets, skin side up, on a rack that will fit inside the smoker. Light the tea leaves with a blow torch, and when smoking place the rack holding the fish on top. Cover and leave to smoke for 30 minutes. Remove the lid and replace the ice and add some more tea leaves, light, cover, and repeat the smoking process again.

5 Remove the fish from the smoker, cool then chill for 4 hours. Use a sharp knife to carve into very thin slices and serve with salad leaves and a little lime pickle. The fish will keep in the refrigerator for up to 3 days.

SERVES 4

10ml/2 tsp salt

10ml/2 tsp sugar

5ml/1 tsp coriander seeds, crushed

3 allspice berries, lightly bruised

5ml/1 tsp dried chilli flakes

5ml/1 tsp chopped fresh dill

500g/1¼lb rainbow trout fillets, skin on

90ml/6 tbsp rooibos tea leaves

baby salad leaves and lime pickle, to serve

Trout gravadlax

Although salmon is the traditional fish used to make gravadlax, sea trout works equally well. Cured in dill, salt and sugar it is simple to prepare and makes a great starter.

1 Freeze the sea trout for at least 24 hours at -20°C (-4°F) and thaw in the refrigerator before commencing the cure. Dry the trout with paper towels.

2 To make the cure, chop most of the the dill finely, using a chef's knife in a steady rocking action, working back and forth until it is very fine and evenly sized. Mix the chopped dill with the salt, sugar and freshly ground black pepper.

3 Scatter a handful of the cure onto the centre of a sheet of clingfilm or plastic wrap, roughly four times the size of the trout fillets. Place one of the fillets skin-side down onto the cure. Reserving another handful of the cure scatter the rest on the surface of the trout fillet and then sandwich the second fillet on top of it, this time skin-side up.

4 Scatter the final handful of the cure on to the top of the trout. Gather the edges of the clingfilm and fold them over to make a small parcel.

5 Place the trout parcel into a dish and put a small weight, such as a plate, on top to gently press it and place in the refrigerator. Turn the parcel over twice each day, at roughly 12 hour intervals. It should be cured for approximately 48 hours; 24 hours at the very least and no more than 36 hours as the fish will become tough and usually very salty. A small quantity of liquid brine will collect around the fish. This is normal and should not be removed as it is essential to get the cure into the trout.

6 When the gravadlax has cured for the required time unwrap the parcel and brush off the excess cure. Only slice the gravadlax once you are ready to serve it. Use a sharp knife and cut it in fine slices at 45° to the length of the fillet. If not using it immediately, wrap in fresh clear film or plastic wrap and keep it covered in the refrigerator for up to three days.

SERVES 4

4 thick sea trout fillets, about 250g/8oz
60g/2½ oz coarse sea salt
15g/1 tbsp sugar
bunch of fresh dill
freshly ground black pepper

Spiced trout salad

SERVES 4

2.5cm/1in piece fresh root ginger, peeled and finely grated

1 garlic clove, crushed

5ml/1 tsp hot chilli powder

15ml/1 tbsp coriander seeds, lightly crushed

grated rind and juice of 2 lemons

60ml/4 tbsp olive oil

450g/1lb trout fillets, skinned

900g/2lb new potatoes

5–10ml/1–2 tsp sea salt

ground black pepper

15ml/1 tbsp whole or chopped fresh chives, to garnish

The trout in this delicious salad is marinated in a mixture of coriander, ginger and chilli and served with cold baby roast potatoes. Make in advance and enjoy at your leisure.

1 Mix the ginger, garlic, chilli powder, coriander seeds and lemon rind in a bowl. Whisk in the lemon juice with 15ml/ 1 tbsp of the olive oil to make a marinade.

2 Place the trout in a dish and cover with the marinade. Turn the fish to make sure they are well coated, cover with clear film or plastic wrap and chill for at least 2 hours or overnight.

3 Preheat the oven to 200°C/400°F/Gas 6. Place the potatoes in a roasting pan, toss them in 30ml/2 tbsp olive oil and season with salt and pepper. Roast for 45 minutes or until tender. Remove from the oven and set aside to cool.

4 Reduce the oven temperature to 190°C/375°F/Gas 5. Remove the trout from the marinade and place in a roasting pan. Bake for 20 minutes or until cooked through. Remove from the oven and leave to cool.

5 Cut the potatoes into chunks, flake the trout into bitesize pieces and toss them together in a serving dish with the remaining olive oil. Sprinkle with the chives and serve.

VARIATION If you don't like spicy hot food, omit the chilli powder in the marinade – the trout tastes equally good without it.

Smoked trout salad

Here horseradish is mixed with yogurt, mustard powder, oil and vinegar to make a piquant salad dressing to perfectly complement the smoked trout.

1 Make the dressing. Mix the mustard powder and white wine vinegar in a bowl, then gradually whisk in the olive oil, yogurt, horseradish and sugar. Set aside for 30 minutes to allow all the flavours to develop.

2 Place the lettuce leaves in a large bowl. Stir the dressing again, then pour half of it over the leaves and toss them lightly using two wooden spoons.

3 Arrange the lettuce on four individual plates with the tomatoes, cucumber and trout. Spoon over the remaining dressing and serve immediately.

COOK'S TIP Fresh grated horseradish varies in potency. If it is too strong, whisk only half the suggested amount into the dressing. If the only horseradish you can find is the creamed variety, you can still use it in the recipe, but mix it with the yogurt first.

SERVES 4

1 oakleaf or other red lettuce

225g/8oz small tomatoes, cut into thin wedges

½ cucumber, peeled and thinly sliced

4 smoked trout fillets, each about 200g/7oz, skinned and flaked

For the dressing

pinch of mustard powder

15–20ml/3–4 tsp white wine vinegar

30ml/2 tbsp light olive oil

100ml/3½fl oz/scant ½ cup natural (plain) yogurt

about 30ml/2 tbsp grated fresh or bottled horseradish

pinch of caster (superfine) sugar

Smoked trout tartlets

Crisp, golden filo pastry contrasts with a creamy trout and three-cheese filling in these pretty little tartlets.

1 Preheat the oven to 180°C/350°F/Gas 4. For each tartlet, place two squares of filo pastry on top of each other at angles to form a star shape. Brush with melted butter and place, buttered side down, in an individual Yorkshire pudding pan or 10cm/4in tartlet pan. Repeat for the other three pans with the remaining filo.

2 Support the pans on a baking sheet and brush the pastry with a little more butter. Bake for 5 minutes or until the tartlets are crisp and light golden brown in colour. Remove the tartlets from the oven but leave the oven on.

3 In a large bowl, combine the three cheeses and milk. Season generously with salt and pepper and mix well.

4 Cut the smoked trout into bitesize pieces using kitchen scissors or a knife. Arrange the halved tomatoes and trout in the pastry cases.

5 Spoon the cheese mixture into the cooked pastry cases, gently pressing it down with the back of a spoon. Return the tartlets to the oven and bake for 10–15 minutes more, until the cheese is bubbling and golden brown. Serve immediately on individual plates, garnished with the parsley and a few salad leaves.

COOK'S TIPS Cover the filo pastry sheets with a damp, clean dishtowel or clear film or plastic wrap until you are ready to use them, so that they do not dry out.
• Although Gruyère is the preferred cheese for these tartlets, Emmenthal or Jarlsberg could be used instead. Grate the cheese finely with a microplane grater.

SERVES 4

8 x 15cm/6in squares filo pastry

50g/2oz/¼ cup butter, melted

50g/2oz Gruyère cheese, grated

115g/4oz/½ cup mascarpone cheese

50g/2oz Parmesan cheese, grated

45ml/3 tbsp milk

75g/3oz smoked trout

8 cherry tomatoes, halved

salt and ground black pepper

fresh flat leaf parsley and salad leaves, to garnish

Seared trout bruschetta

SERVES 4-8

1 baguette
1 garlic clove, halved
30ml/2 tbsp extra virgin olive oil
120ml/4fl oz/½ cup crème fraîche or sour cream
15ml/1 tbsp creamed horseradish
15ml/1 tbsp chopped fresh chives
4 trout fillets, each about 115g/4oz
50g/2oz watercress, land cress or salad leaves
salt and ground black pepper
lemon juice and extra virgin olive oil, to serve

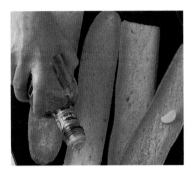

These resemble open sandwiches and are hearty enough to make a satisfying lunchtime snack for four people. If you prefer, cut the baguette into eight and serve as an appetizer.

1 Preheat the grill or broiler to high and preheat the oven to 150°C/300°F/Gas 2. Cut the baguette in half horizontally, then cut each half vertically to give four equal-sized pieces.

2 Toast the bread under the grill or broiler until lightly browned. Rub the toasted bread all over with the halved garlic clove and drizzle with olive oil. Keep warm in the oven while you prepare the topping.

3 In a small bowl, mix the crème fraîche or sour cream, horseradish and chives with salt and pepper to taste.

4 Season the trout fillets lightly and brush over a little olive oil. Heat a frying pan until really hot and add the trout, placing the fillets skin-side down. Sear for 3 minutes, flip over and cook for 30 seconds more.

5 Place one seared trout fillet on each piece of toasted baguette. Add a generous dollop of the horseradish cream and some watercress, land cress or salad leaves. Serve drizzled with lemon juice and extra olive oil.

Hot trout sandwich

This Mediterranean-style sandwich is so easy to prepare and makes a tasty weekend lunch. Choose your favourite bread, but make sure it is really fresh.

1 Preheat the oven to 180°C/350°F/Gas 4. Place the peppers and tomatoes in a roasting pan and drizzle half the olive oil over. Bake for 25–30 minutes or until the pepper skins are blackened. Set aside to cool.

2 In a small bowl, whisk the remaining oil with the lemon juice and a little salt and freshly ground black pepper. Place the trout in a shallow, non-metallic dish and pour over the oil and lemon juice. Turn the fish to make sure they are well coated.

3 Peel the skin off the cooked peppers and discard the core and seeds. Cut the pepper flesh into strips. Slice each ciabatta loaf in half vertically, then cut each half in half horizontally.

4 Heat a ridged griddle pan over a medium heat. Lift the trout fillets carefully out of the marinade and fry them for 1–2 minutes, without adding any oil, until just cooked.

5 Mix the pesto and mayonnaise together and spread over the bread. Divide the rocket among four halves of the bread and top with the trout fillet, pepper strips and roasted tomatoes. Place the remaining bread on top and serve.

COOK'S TIPS Small loaves of olive-oil bread, such as ciabatta and focaccia, are ideal for these sandwiches. Try the sun-dried tomato and black olive versions, too, if you like.
• If you can't find any red pesto, use 30ml/2 tbsp chopped fresh basil mixed with 15ml/1 tbsp sun-dried tomato paste.

SERVES 4–6

2 red (bell) peppers
8 cherry tomatoes
60ml/4 tbsp extra virgin olive oil
30ml/2 tbsp lemon juice
4 trout fillets, each about 115g/4oz, skinned
2 small ciabatta loaves
15ml/1 tbsp red pesto
30ml/2 tbsp mayonnaise
115g/4oz rocket (arugula)
salt and ground black pepper

Goat's cheese and trout toasties

SERVES 4

8 thick slices of white bread

30ml/2 tbsp olive oil

5ml/1 tsp fresh thyme leaves

20ml/4 tsp pesto

50g/2oz smoked trout, sliced

4 round goat's cheese slices, each about 50g/2oz

salt and ground black pepper

These little rounds are packed full of flavour – the goat's cheese and trout combine beautifully to make a tasty snack suitable for any time of the day.

1 Preheat the oven to 200°C/400°F/Gas 6. Using a pastry cutter that is slightly larger than the goat's cheese rounds, cut a circle from each slice of bread.

2 Brush the bread rounds with a little olive oil, scatter with a few thyme leaves and season well. Place the bread rounds on a baking sheet and bake for 5 minutes or until crisp and a light golden colour.

3 Remove the bread from the oven and spread 5ml/1 tsp pesto over half the rounds. Divide the smoked trout among the pesto-topped bread, top with the cheese rounds and season well with black pepper. Top the cheese with the remaining bread circles.

4 Bake the toasties in the oven for 5 minutes more, until the cheese has just started to soften slightly. Remove from the oven and serve immediately.

VARIATIONS Thyme goes particularly well with goat's cheese but other strong herbs can be substituted. Try oregano, marjoram or sage for a completely different taste.
• For a milder flavour, use rounds of under-ripe Brie or Camembert cheese in place of the goat's cheese.

Cheese scones with trout butter

These moreish scones are topped with a richly flavoured smoked trout and horseradish butter, which can be prepared a day ahead. The cheese scones are best baked on the day you are planning to eat them as they stale quite quickly.

1 Make the smoked trout butter. Place the softened butter, smoked trout and creamed horseradish in a food processor. Season to taste with salt and ground black pepper. Process the ingredients until well blended. Transfer to a bowl, cover and chill until needed.

2 Preheat the oven to 220°C/425°F/Gas 7. To make the scones, sift the flours and baking powder into a mixing bowl. Season the flour with salt and ground black pepper.

3 Rub the butter into the flour with your fingertips until the mixture resembles fine breadcrumbs. Stir in most of the grated cheese, reserving just enough to sprinkle on top of the scones.

4 Stir in the beaten egg and enough milk to make a smooth, soft dough. Knead the dough gently and turn it out on a floured surface. Roll or pat the dough out to a thickness of 2cm/¾in. Using a plain 7.5cm/3in cutter, stamp out six scones.

5 Place the scones on a well-greased baking sheet, brush with a little milk to glaze and sprinkle the reserved cheese over. Bake for 15–20 minutes or until just turning golden. Cool slightly on a wire rack.

6 Remove the smoked trout butter from the refrigerator 30 minutes before serving. Split the warm scones in half, top with the butter and serve.

COOK'S TIP For lighter scones, handle the dough as little as possible, mixing the ingredients together quickly and kneading the dough as briefly as possible. Sifting the flours into the mixing bowl from a height will help to incorporate additional air into the scone mixture.

MAKES 6

75g/3oz/¾ cup self-raising (self-rising) flour

75g/3oz/¾ cup plain (all-purpose) flour

5ml/1 tsp baking powder

25g/1oz/2 tbsp butter

75g/3oz Cheddar cheese or Monterey Jack, grated

1 egg, beaten

45ml/3 tbsp milk

salt and ground black pepper

For the trout butter

50g/2oz/¼ cup butter, softened

50g/2oz smoked trout, flaked

5ml/1 tsp creamed horseradish

Smoked trout soufflé omelette

SERVES 1

2 eggs, separated
30ml/2 tbsp water
25g/1oz/2 tbsp butter
15ml/1 tbsp chopped fresh parsley
15ml/1 tbsp chopped fresh chives
50g/2oz smoked trout, roughly chopped
40g/1½oz Gruyère cheese, finely grated
salt and ground black pepper
warm bread, to serve

For the tomato and basil salad

3 plum tomatoes, sliced
30ml/2 tbsp fresh basil leaves
5ml/1 tsp balsamic vinegar
15ml/1 tbsp extra virgin olive oil

Half omelette, half soufflé, this light supper dish is the ideal choice for when you're just cooking for yourself. Packed with fresh herbs and smoked trout, it is full of flavour. Serve it simply with a glass of dry white wine, some warm country bread and a fresh salad, such as basil and tomato.

1 Make the salad. Arrange the tomato slices on a serving plate and top with the fresh basil leaves. Drizzle the vinegar and oil over and season well. Set aside but do not chill, as the sweet flavour of the tomatoes will be more pronounced at room temperature.

2 Put the egg whites in a mixing bowl and add salt and pepper. Using a hand-held electric mixer or rotary whisk, whisk until they are stiff but not dry. In a separate mixing bowl, whisk the egg yolks with the water until creamy.

3 Using a large metal spoon, add a little of the egg white mixture to the yolks. Fold in carefully to incorporate as much air as possible. Add the remaining white and fold in gently.

4 Preheat the grill or broiler to high. Melt the butter in an 18cm/7in frying pan which can safely be used under the grill. Swirl the pan around to grease the sides thoroughly.

5 Pour the egg mixture into the pan and cook over a medium heat, gently shivering the pan from time to time, until the omelette is golden brown on the base and just firm to the touch in the centre.

6 Sprinkle over the herbs, smoked trout and grated cheese.

7 Place the pan under the grill and cook until the egg is just set and the cheese is golden and bubbling. Run a blunt knife around the edge of the pan to release the omelette, then gently score a line right across the centre of the omelette.

8 Fold the omelette in half and slide it carefully on to a hot serving plate. Serve immediately with the tomato and basil salad and warm bread.

Trout-filled pittas with mustard mayo

SERVES 4

175g/6oz hot smoked trout fillets

6 sun-dried tomatoes in oil, drained and finely chopped

90ml/6 tbsp mayonnaise

10ml/2 tsp wholegrain mustard

4 pitta breads

2 Little Gem (Bibb) lettuces

1 yellow (bell) pepper, finely diced

salt and ground black pepper

Mustard and trout may not be an obvious combination but they taste great when teamed together in these pitta breads.

1 Preheat the oven to 180°C/350°F/Gas 4. To make the filling, flake the trout into small pieces and place in a large bowl.

2 Add the chopped sun-dried tomatoes, mayonnaise and mustard to the trout. Season to taste with salt and plenty of ground black pepper.

3 Wrap the pitta breads in foil and heat them in the oven for 10 minutes.

4 Shred the lettuces and mix with the yellow pepper in a bowl.

5 Remove the pitta breads from the oven and split each one along one side with a sharp knife. Half fill each pitta with the lettuce and pepper mixture. Add one quarter of the trout mixture and season well before serving.

MAIN MEALS

Trout is a very versatile fish that marries well with a range of flavours such as Trout with Tamarind and Chilli Sauce or Poached Trout with Fennel. It looks fabulous when served whole, whether stuffed with delicious herbs and spices or luxuriatingly wrapped in succulent prosciutto. However you serve trout, it will look and taste fantastic.

Baked trout with a gremolata crust

SERVES 4–6

1 small aubergine
(eggplant),
cubed
1 red (bell) pepper, diced
1 yellow (bell) pepper, diced
1 small red onion, chopped
30ml/2 tbsp olive oil
350g/12oz trout fillets
juice of 1 lime
salt and ground black
pepper
chunks of bread, to serve

For the gremolata crust
grated rind of 1 lemon
grated rind of 1 lime
25g/1oz/½ cup fresh
breadcrumbs
30ml/2 tbsp chopped fresh
flat leaf parsley
1 garlic clove, finely
chopped

A gremolata crust is a combination of breadcrumbs with finely chopped parsley, lemon rind and garlic.

1 Preheat the oven to 200°C/400°F/Gas 6. Place the aubergine, peppers and onion in a roasting pan. Add the oil and stir to coat. Sprinkle with salt and pepper. Cook for 40 minutes or until the edges of the vegetables have begun to char.

2 Make the gremolata by mixing the lemon and lime rind with the breadcrumbs, chopped parsley and garlic. Season.

3 Place the trout fillets on top of the vegetables in the roasting pan and cover the surface of the fish with the breadcrumb mixture. Return to the oven for a further 15 minutes or until the fish is fully cooked and the gremolata topping is crunchy.

4 Divide the fish and vegetables among four serving plates and sprinkle the lime juice over to taste. Serve with bread to soak up all the juices.

Chinese-style steamed trout

If you think steamed trout sounds dull, think again. This fish, marinated in a black bean, ginger and garlic mixture before being moistened with rice wine and soy sauce, is superb.

1 Wash the fish inside and out under cold running water, then pat dry on kitchen paper. Using a sharp knife, slash 3–4 deep crosses on either side of each fish.

2 Place half the black beans and the sugar in a small bowl and mash together with the back of a fork. When the beans are thoroughly mashed, stir in the remaining whole beans.

3 Place a little ginger and garlic inside the cavity of each fish, then lay them on a plate or dish that will fit inside a large steamer. Rub the bean mixture into the fish, working it into the slashes, then sprinkle the remaining ginger and garlic over the top. Cover with clear film or plastic wrap and place the fish in the refrigerator for at least 30 minutes.

4 Remove the fish from the refrigerator and place the steamer over a pan of boiling water. Sprinkle the rice wine or sherry and half the soy sauce over the fish and place the plate of fish inside the steamer. Steam for 15–20 minutes, or until the fish is cooked and the flesh flakes easily when tested with a fork.

5 Using a fish slice or metal spatula, carefully lift the fish on to a warmed serving dish. Sprinkle the fish with the remaining soy sauce, then sprinkle with the shredded or sliced spring onions.

6 In a small pan, heat the groundnut oil until very hot and smoking, then trickle it over the spring onions and fish. Lightly sprinkle the sesame oil over the fish and serve immediately.

SERVES 6

2 whole trout, each about 675–800g/1½–1¾lb, cleaned

25ml/1½ tbsp salted black beans

2.5ml/½ tsp granulated sugar

30ml/2 tbsp finely shredded fresh root ginger

4 garlic cloves, thinly sliced

30ml/2 tbsp Chinese rice wine or dry sherry

30ml/2 tbsp light soy sauce

4–6 spring onions (scallions), finely shredded or sliced diagonally

45ml/3 tbsp groundnut (peanut) oil

10ml/2 tsp sesame oil

Trout with tamarind and chilli sauce

SERVES 4

4 whole trout, each about 350g/12oz, cleaned

6 spring onions (scallions), sliced

60ml/4 tbsp soy sauce

15ml/1 tbsp groundnut (peanut) oil

2 red chillies, cut into fine strips

30ml/2 tbsp chopped fresh coriander (cilantro)

For the sauce

50g/2oz tamarind pulp

105ml/7 tbsp boiling water

2 shallots, roughly chopped

1 fresh red chilli, seeded and chopped

1cm/½in piece fresh root ginger, peeled and chopped

5ml/1 tsp soft brown sugar

45ml/3 tbsp Thai fish sauce

This spicy Thai-inspired sauce really gives this dish a zing. If you like your food very spicy, add an extra chilli.

1 Wash the fish inside and out under cold running water, then pat dry with kitchen paper. Slash each trout diagonally four or five times on either side with a sharp knife. Place in one or two shallow dishes.

2 Fill the cavities with spring onions. Douse each fish on both sides with soy sauce, turning the fish over carefully. Sprinkle on any remaining spring onions and set aside until required.

3 Make the sauce. Put the tamarind pulp in a small bowl and pour on the boiling water. Mash with a fork until soft. Tip into a food processor or blender and add the shallots, fresh chilli, ginger, sugar and fish sauce. Whizz to a coarse pulp.

4 Heat the oil in a large frying pan or wok and fry the trout, one at a time if necessary, for about 5 minutes on each side, until the skin is crisp and browned and the flesh cooked. Put on warmed plates and spoon over some sauce. Sprinkle with the chilli and coriander and serve.

Smoked trout with horseradish sauce

The combination of cold horseradish sauce and smoked trout has been classic across Europe for hundreds of years.

1 Place the smoked trout in a small dish, add water to cover and soak for 30 minutes. Drain and pat dry with kitchen paper.

2 Divide the lamb's lettuce among four plates. Place the cress around the edges of the plates and add the radishes. Arrange the trout strips, lamb's lettuce, parsley and shrimps in the centre of the plate.

3 Top each plate with two anchovy fillets and garnish with lemon wedges.

4 Mix together the horseradish and mayonnaise in a bowl and season to taste with salt and pepper.

5 Serve the smoked fish with the horseradish sauce and with toast and butter.

SERVES 4

300g/11oz smoked trout fillets, skinned and cut into strips

150g/5oz lamb's lettuce

60ml/4 tbsp cress

2 radishes, sliced

30ml/2 tbsp fresh parsley, very finely chopped

50g/2oz/½ cup cooked shrimp

8 canned anchovy fillets, drained

15ml/1 tbsp grated horseradish

30ml/2 tbsp mayonnaise

salt and ground black pepper

lemon wedges, to garnish

toasted white bread and butter, to serve

Trout baked in white wine with buttered almonds

Sweet-flavoured, white-fleshed trout tastes wonderful when baked simply. This traditional preparation with flaked almonds is a winner every time. Serve with roasted leeks, if you like.

1 Preheat the oven to 180°C/350°F/Gas 4. Season the trout and put on a baking tray. Place the onion inside the fish and pour over the wine. Add the bay leaves, herbs, peppercorns and lemon wedges to the tray. Cover the tray with foil. Bake for 30 minutes.

2 Take out of the oven and carefully remove the foil, making sure that you do not scald yourself with the escaping steam. Keep the fish warm and pour the cooking liquid into a small pan.

3 Put the pan over medium-high heat and cook for 5–8 minutes to reduce the liquid slightly. Adjust the seasoning.

4 Meanwhile, melt the butter in a small pan and add the almonds. Cook for 3–4 minutes, or until the almonds are golden and crispy.

5 Serve the trout with the almonds on top, accompanied by the reduced cooking juices.

SERVES 4

4 whole trout, each about 200g/7oz each, cleaned and head on

1 red onion, sliced into rings

300ml/½ pint/1¼ cups white wine

2 bay leaves

2–3 sprigs each of fresh parsley, thyme and rosemary

4–5 black peppercorns

½ lemon, cut into wedges

15g/½oz/1 tbsp butter

45ml/3 tbsp flaked (sliced) almonds

salt and ground black pepper

Trout with cucumber cream

SERVES 4

25g/1oz/2 tbsp butter

8 trout fillets, each about 100g/3½oz, skinned

2 large spring onions (scallions), white parts only, chopped

½ cucumber, peeled, seeded and cut into short batons

5ml/1 tsp cornflour (cornstarch)

150ml/¼ pint/⅔ cup single (light) cream

50ml/2fl oz/¼ cup dry sherry

30ml/2 tbsp chopped fresh tarragon

1 tomato, halved, seeded and chopped

salt and ground black pepper

new potatoes and green beans, to serve

Cream sauces suit the delicate flavour of trout very well. This one introduces two more complementary elements, cucumber and tarragon.

1 Melt the butter in a large frying pan. Season the trout fillets, place in the pan and cook for 6 minutes, turning once. Transfer to a warm plate, cover and keep warm.

2 Add the spring onions and cucumber to the butter remaining in the pan. Cook over a gentle heat, stirring, until soft but not coloured.

3 Put the cornflour in a cup and stir in about 30ml/2 tbsp of the cream to make a thin paste.

4 Add the remaining cream to the pan. Stir in the cornflour mixture and the sherry. Heat, stirring constantly, until the mixture thickens.

5 Stir in the chopped tarragon. Add the chopped tomato with a little salt and pepper, to taste. Stir until the sauce is thoroughly combined.

6 Place the trout fillets on warmed serving plates. Spoon the sauce over and serve the fish with boiled new potatoes and green beans.

Thai-style trout

The combination of classic Thai aromatic ingredients – ginger, lemon grass, coconut milk and lime – gives this simple dish a fabulous flavour. Serve with plenty of steamed Thai fragrant rice to soak up the delicious sauce.

1 Preheat the oven to 200°C/400°F/Gas 6. Place the spinach in a pan, with just the water that adheres to the leaves after washing. Cover with a lid and cook gently for 3–4 minutes until the leaves have just wilted. Drain the spinach in a colander and press it with the back of a spoon to remove any excess moisture.

2 Transfer the spinach to a mixing bowl and stir in the chopped lemon grass, grated ginger and garlic.

3 Combine the coconut milk, lime juice, sugar and seasoning in a jug or pitcher. Place the trout fillets side by side in a shallow baking dish and pour the coconut milk mixture over.

4 Bake the trout for 20–25 minutes until cooked. Place on individual serving plates, on top of the steamed Thai fragrant rice. Toss the spinach mixture in the juices remaining in the dish, spoon on top of the fish and serve.

COOK'S TIP To steam Thai fragrant rice, cook it in a pan of salted boiling water for three-quarters of the time noted on the packet. Transfer it to a colander lined with muslin or cheesecloth and steam over simmering water for 5–10 minutes until just tender.

SERVES 4

200g/7oz spinach leaves

1 lemon grass stalk, finely chopped

2.5cm/1in piece fresh root ginger, peeled and finely grated

2 garlic cloves, crushed

200ml/7fl oz/scant 1 cup coconut milk

30ml/2 tbsp freshly squeezed lime juice

15ml/1 tbsp soft light brown sugar

4 trout fillets, each about 200g/7oz

salt and ground black pepper

steamed Thai fragrant rice, to serve

Trout with crunchy peppercorns

Black, green and pink peppercorns add colour and texture to this dish, and provide an explosion of taste in the mouth when crunched. Serve the trout fillets with creamy mashed potatoes swirled with pesto.

1 Place the mixed peppercorns in a mortar and crush them lightly with a pestle. Continue until about half the peppercorns are broken.

2 Press one-quarter of the peppercorns on to the flesh of each trout fillet, using the back of a spoon.

3 Heat the oil in a griddle pan. Place the fish in the pan, coated-side up, and fry for 2–3 minutes, using a spatula to press the peppercorns further into the fish as it cooks.

4 Using the spatula, turn the trout fillets over and cook for 2–3 minutes more, until cooked right through. Turn the fillets over again in the pan and sprinkle with the lemon juice.

5 Place each fish on a bed of pesto mash on an individual plate and garnish with the basil sprigs.

COOK'S TIP Stir a large spoonful of pesto into the mashed potato just before serving, leaving green swirls in the creamy potato.

SERVES 4

60ml/4 tbsp mixed peppercorns

4 trout fillets, each about 200g/7oz

60ml/4 tbsp olive oil

juice of 1 lemon

fresh basil sprigs, to garnish

mashed potato with pesto, to serve

Stuffed trout with tarragon sauce

SERVES 4

90ml/6 tbsp fresh white breadcrumbs

30ml/2 tbsp chopped fresh tarragon, plus extra sprigs

1 egg, beaten

4 whole trout, each about 200g/7oz, cleaned and boned for stuffing

1 small onion, sliced

150ml/¼ pint/⅔ cup dry white wine

25g/1oz/2 tbsp butter

15ml/1 tbsp plain (all-purpose) flour

150ml/¼ pint/⅔ cup single (light) cream

salt and ground black pepper

lime wedges, new potatoes, and a selection of steamed green vegetables, to serve

Taragon and trout make a marvellous team. Here whole trout are filled with a herby stuffing before being baked in wine and served with a creamy tarragon sauce. Removing the skin before serving reveals the attractive pale pink trout flesh.

1 Preheat the oven to 190°C/375°F/Gas 5. Mix the breadcrumbs with half the chopped tarragon in a bowl. Season with salt and pepper, then bind the mixture together with the beaten egg.

2 Spread a layer of tarragon stuffing inside the cavity of each trout, pressing the mixture down firmly to mould it to the shape of the cavity. Season the trout well.

3 Place the trout in a single layer in a shallow baking dish. Add the onion slices and wine to the dish and top each fish with a sprig of tarragon.Cover the dish tightly with foil. Bake for 20–25 minutes or until tender.

4 Carefully remove the cooked trout from the dish, reserving the cooking liquid. Remove the heads, tails and skin, then place the fish in a hot ovenproof dish. Cover with foil and keep warm in the oven.

5 Strain the cooking liquid into a measuring jug or cup and if necessary make up with water to give 150ml/¼ pint/⅔ cup of liquid.

6 Melt the butter in a pan, stir in the flour and cook, stirring constantly, for 1–2 minutes. Gradually add the cooking liquid, stirring constantly. Add the cream in the same way and bring to the boil. Continue to stir as the mixture thickens to a smooth sauce. Season with salt and black pepper and add the remaining chopped tarragon.

7 Place the trout on four warmed plates and pour over the tarragon sauce. Serve with lime wedges, buttered new potatoes, and steamed green vegetables.

Trout fillets in a creamy mustard sauce

This is a light, tasty dish that is perfect for a mid-week meal or lunch with friends. The mustard sauce is made with grainy mustard to add texture to the dish. Fried potatoes with bacon are a perfect accompaniment.

1 Heat the fish stock and season it, if necessary, with salt and pepper. Add the cream and mustard and simmer for 5 minutes to make the sauce.

2 Heat some oil in a frying pan over high heat and fry the potato slices and the bacon until browned and crisp. Add the onion and fry for another 5 minutes. Season with salt and pepper and stir in the chives.

3 Meanwhile, season the fish with lemon juice, salt and pepper. Heat some oil in another pan and fry the fillets, turning once, until golden on both sides. Arrange the fried potatoes in the middle of a serving plate with the fish round them and pour the sauce around. Garnish with fresh dill.

COOK'S TIP If the sauce seems too thin, thicken it with about 5ml/ 1 tsp cornflour or cornstarch slaked in a little cold water.

SERVES 4

300ml/½ pint/1¼ cups fish stock

100ml/3½oz/scant ½ cup single (light) cream

10ml/2 tsp grainy mustard

1kg/2¼lb boiled potatoes, thinly sliced

150g/5oz bacon, diced into cubes

1 onion, finely chopped

small bunch chives, chopped

4 trout fillets, each about 200g/7oz

juice of 1 lemon

oil, for frying

salt and ground white pepper

fresh dill, to garnish

Whole glazed trout with cucumber salad

SERVES 4

1 whole trout, total weight about 1.5kg/3¼lb, cleaned
1 bay leaf
1 bunch fresh parsley
30ml/2 tbsp salt
10 black peppercorns
1 lemon, sliced
1 packet powdered aspic
500ml/17fl oz/2¼ cups clear fish stock or water
salt and ground white pepper
fresh dill or parsley sprigs, to garnish

For the cucumber salad
1 cucumber
105ml/7 tbsp fresh lemon juice or white wine vinegar
105ml/7 tbsp water
30–45ml/2–3 tbsp sugar
30ml/2 tbsp chopped fresh parsley
salt and ground black pepper

The presentation of the trout in this recipe looks splendid, and the sweet-sour cucumber salad is a great accompaniment. A whole salmon can be prepared in the same way.

1 Put the fish in a fish kettle or, if not possible, bend the fish into a semi-circle to fit a suitably sized pan, with the backbone uppermost. Add enough water to just cover the fish.

2 Tie the bay leaf and parsley together with string. Add to the pan with the salt, peppercorns and half the lemon slices.

3 Bring slowly to the boil and then simmer for 1 minute. Remove the pan from the heat but leave the fish in the cooking liquid. Set the pan aside, in a cool place, until the fish is cold.

4 Meanwhile, prepare the cucumber for the salad. Peel the skin off the cucumber if you prefer. Otherwise the skin can be left on or scored down its length with a fork. Slice it finely. Put the sliced cucumber in a colander, sprinkling each layer generously with salt. Put a saucer then a weight on top and leave to drain for 1–2 hours.

5 To make the dressing, mix together the lemon juice or vinegar, water, sugar to taste, pepper and a pinch of salt if necessary. Stir well to dissolve the sugar.

6 Dissolve the aspic powder in the stock or water, according to packet instructions. Check the seasoning and add salt and pepper to taste only if necessary.

7 Carefully remove the fish from the stock and place on a serving dish. Gently ease the skin off the fish; leave the head and tail intact. Remove the fat from along the backbone. Allow to drain completely, then dry with kitchen paper.

8 As the aspic begins to thicken, brush it over the whole trout. Leave to set. Garnish with dill or parsley sprigs and the remaining lemon slices. Rinse the cucumber under cold running water then squeeze dry. Put in a serving dish and pour over the dressing. Sprinkle over the parsley and serve with the fish.

Poached trout with fennel

Cooking trout, fennel and potatoes together in one dish makes for an easy supper – simply add your favourite steamed green vegetables to complete the meal.

1 Preheat the oven to 180°C/350°F/Gas 4. Cut the feathery green fronds from the fennel, chop very finely and set aside. Slice the fennel bulb thinly.

2 Grease a shallow baking dish with butter and spread out the fennel bulb slices to cover the base of the dish.

3 Spread out the potato slices on top of the fennel and top with the bay leaf. Pour the vermouth and water over the vegetables. Season to taste.

4 Cover the dish tightly with foil and bake in the oven for 35–40 minutes.

5 Remove the dish from the oven and lift off the foil. Place the trout on top of the vegetables and dot with butter. Replace the foil and bake for 20–25 minutes more, until the trout are cooked and the vegetables are tender.

6 Remove the foil and sprinkle the reserved chopped fennel over the fish. Serve immediately, with steamed green vegetables.

COOK'S TIP Dry vermouth has a concentrated flavour that works very well in this recipe, and the herbs that are an intrinsic part of it are more than a match for the robust flavour of the fennel.

SERVES 2

1 small fennel bulb, about 175g/6oz, with fronds

25g/1oz/2 tbsp butter, plus extra for greasing

350g/12oz potatoes, peeled and thinly sliced

1 bay leaf

60ml/4 tbsp dry vermouth

60ml/4 tbsp water

2 whole trout, each about 225g/8oz, cleaned

salt and ground black pepper

steamed green vegetables, to serve

Garlic baked trout with avocado salad

Packed full of flavour and plenty of vitamins and minerals, this baked trout is a versatile main dish. Serve it as soon as the trout comes out of the oven, with new potatoes, or cold with country bread. If the latter, dress the salad just before serving.

1 Preheat the oven to 180°C/350°F/Gas 4. Place the tomatoes on a baking tray lined with baking parchment.

2 Sprinkle the garlic and basil over the tomatoes and season well with black pepper. Drizzle 15ml/1 tbsp of the olive oil over and bake for 25 minutes. Remove from the oven.

3 Move the tomato halves closer together, if necessary, to make room for the trout. Place the fillets on the baking tray. Return the tray to the oven for a further 15 minutes.

4 Test the fish with a fork to check it is cooked through: if the flesh flakes easily it is ready. Remove the tray from the oven.

5 Meanwhile, cut the avocados in half, remove the stone (pit) and peel, then slice the flesh lengthways into fine pieces.

6 In a small bowl, whisk the lime juice with the remaining olive oil. Season the dressing with salt and plenty of black pepper.

7 Divide the watercress, land cress or rocket among four individual serving plates. Top with the avocado slices. Drizzle the lime dressing over.

8 Using a fish slice, lift the cooked trout fillets carefully off the baking tray and place them on a board.

9 Arrange the cooked tomatoes over the salad leaves and pour over any cooking juices that have accumulated on the baking parchment.

10 Flake the trout into bitesize pieces and divide among the plates, arranging it amongst the salad leaves. Garnish the plates with the lime wedges and serve, with new potatoes.

SERVES 4

6 plum tomatoes, halved

2 garlic cloves, thinly sliced

15g/½oz/½ cup fresh basil leaves

45ml/3 tbsp olive oil

4 trout fillets, each about 200g/7oz, skinned

2 avocados

juice of 1 lime

75g/3oz watercress, land cress or rocket (arugula)

salt and ground black pepper

new potatoes, to serve

lime wedges, to garnish

Stuffed trout with orange sauce

Stuffing trout with mushrooms and parsley not only adds a new flavour dimension but also makes the meal more substantial. Tangy orange sauce is a perfect accompaniment.

1 Remove the heads and gills from the trout. Rinse the cavities thoroughly and bone the fish to make them easier to stuff.

2 Preheat the oven to 190°C/375°F/Gas 5. Melt the butter in a small pan, and fry the onion over a medium heat for 4–5 minutes until translucent.

3 Add the mushrooms to the pan and fry for a further minute. Remove from the heat and stir in the breadcrumbs, parsley and egg. Season with plenty of salt and black pepper.

4 Stuff each trout with one-quarter of the mixture, pressing the mixture firmly to distribute evenly and enclose it securely in the fish.

5 Season the trout well and place in a single layer in a shallow baking dish. Pour over the orange juice. Cover the dish with foil. Cook for 20–25 minutes or until the trout are cooked through.

6 Meanwhile, make the sauce. Melt the butter in a frying pan and add the sugar. Add the orange slices to the pan and brown on both sides. Add the orange and lemon juice and stir well. Cook for 2–3 minutes, then remove from the heat.

7 Carefully lift the cooked trout out of the dish, reserving the cooking liquid. Place the fish on a hot serving dish, cover with foil and keep warm in the oven.

8 Add the cooking liquid to the sauce in the frying pan and stir well. Garnish the stuffed trout with the orange slices and dill sprigs, then pour the orange sauce over and serve.

SERVES 4

4 whole trout, each about 175g/6oz, cleaned

25g/1oz/2 tbsp butter

1 small onion, finely chopped

50g/2oz/¾ cup button (white) mushrooms, chopped

25g/1oz/½ cup fresh white breadcrumbs

30ml/2 tbsp chopped fresh parsley

1 egg, beaten

juice of 2 oranges

salt and ground black pepper

fresh dill sprigs, to garnish

For the orange sauce

25g/1oz/2 tbsp butter

pinch of caster (superfine) sugar

1 orange, thinly sliced

juice of 1 orange

juice of ½ lemon

Trout with prosciutto

SERVES 4-6

4 whole brown or rainbow trout, each about 250g/9oz, cleaned

16 thin slices prosciutto, about 200g/7oz

50g/2oz/¼ cup melted butter, plus extra for greasing

salt and ground black pepper

roasted potatoes, to serve

Fresh trout is often cooked with simple flavourings as in this recipe, so that the delicious and delicate flavour of the fish shines through. Serve with roasted potatoes.

1 Extend the belly cavity of each trout, cutting up one side of the backbone. Slip a knife behind the rib bones to loosen them (sometimes just flexing the fish makes them pop up). Snip these off from both sides with scissors, and season the fish well inside.

2 Preheat the grill or broiler to high, with a shelf in the top position. Line a baking tray with foil and butter it.

3 Working with the fish on the foil, fold a piece of prosciutto into each belly. Use smaller or broken bits of prosciutto for this, and reserve the eight best slices.

4 Brush each trout with a little butter, seasoning the outside lightly with salt and pepper. Wrap two prosciutto slices round each one, crossways, tucking the ends into the belly. Grill or broil the trout for 4 minutes, then carefully turn them over with a metal spatula, rolling them across on the belly, so that the prosciutto doesn't come loose, and grill for a further 4 minutes.

5 Serve the trout very hot, with any spare butter spooned over the top. Diners should open the trout on their plates, and eat them from the inside, pushing the flesh off the skin.

Rainbow trout in lemon and mustard marinade

In this recipe, whole trout are marinated in a mixture of mustard oil, chilli, lemon juice and rind. They are then baked and served with a spicy hot seasoning poured over the top. This dish is fabulous served with basmati rice.

1 Lay the fish on a flat surface and make three diagonal slits on each side. Put them in a shallow dish. Mix the marinade ingredients together and pour over the fish. Gently rub in the marinade, working it well into the slits. Set aside for 1 hour.

2 Preheat the oven to 180⁰C/350⁰F/Gas Mark 4. Line a roasting pan with foil and brush it generously with oil. Lay the fish in the pan and cook in the centre of the oven for 20 minutes.

3 For the sauce, heat the oil over a medium heat. When it is smoking, remove the pan from the heat and add the mustard seeds, then the onion. Fry the onion until translucent.

4 Add the crushed chilli and cook for 1 minute. Pour in 120ml/4floz/½ cup warm water and cook it for 2–3 minutes. Transfer the fish to a serving dish.

5 Add the fish juices to the onion sauce, then stir in the chopped coriander and cook for 1 minute. Spoon the sauce over the fish and serve with plain basmati rice and lemon wedges.

SERVES 4

4 whole rainbow trout, each about 250g/9oz, cleaned

basmati rice and lemon wedges, to serve

For the marinade

60ml/4 tbsp mustard oil

5ml/1 tsp salt or to taste

5ml/1 tsp fennel seeds

2.5ml/½ tsp crushed dried chilli

grated rind and juice of 1 lemon

2.5ml/½ tsp ground turmeric

For the sauce

30ml/2 tbsp mustard oil

2.5ml/½ tsp mustard seeds

1 medium onion, finely chopped

2.5ml/½ tsp crushed dried chilli

45ml/3 tbsp chopped fresh coriander (cilantro) leaves

Baked trout with caraway

Caraway seeds is another classic accompaniment to trout. For the best flavour cook the trout the day it has been caught. Serve with plenty of roasted garlicky new potatoes.

1 Season each fish with 5ml/1 tsp salt and 15ml/1 tbsp caraway seeds on the inside and outside. Preheat the oven to 180°C/350°F/Gas 4.

2 Cook the potatoes in salted boiling water for 6 minutes. Drain and cut the larger potatoes in half.

3 Mix the garlic with the olive oil and pour over the potatoes. Shake the pan to cover the potatoes with the oil, and transfer to a roasting pan. Season with salt and sprinkle over the rosemary.

4 Make the tartare sauce by mixing the mayonnaise with the onion and gherkin. Transfer to a serving bowl and chill.

5 Cut half the butter into slices and spread it over an ovenproof dish that will fit the trout. Add the fish and cover with slices of the remaining butter.

6 Roast the potatoes on the top shelf of the oven for 25 minutes, or until golden and crispy, turning at least once during cooking. Bake the fish on the centre shelf for 30 minutes.

7 Serve the trout with a slice of lemon and some tartare sauce for the potatoes.

SERVES 4

4 whole trout, each about 250g/9oz, cleaned

4 tsp salt

60ml/4 tbsp caraway seeds

115g/4oz/½ cup butter

1 lemon, sliced, to serve

For the new potatoes

800g/1¾lb new potatoes, unpeeled and left whole

3 garlic cloves, peeled and crushed

45ml/3 tbsp olive oil

salt

1 sprig fresh rosemary, torn

For the tartare sauce

45ml/3 tbsp mayonnaise

1 small onion, peeled and diced into small pieces

1 gherkin, finely chopped

Trout with orange and herbs

SERVES 4

4 whole trout, each about
275g/10oz, cleaned

4 oranges

60ml/4 tbsp olive oil

½ bunch fresh dill

½ bunch fresh thyme

few sprigs of fresh rosemary

few sprigs of fresh parsley

sea salt and ground black
pepper

rocket (arugula), beetroot
(beet), toasted flaked
almonds, and crusty bread
and butter, to serve

This light and refreshing recipe is just perfect for an alfresco lunch. Fragrant oranges and fresh herbs are used to enhance the delicate flavour of the trout.

1 Preheat the oven to 180°C/350°F/Gas 4. Make three diagonal cuts on each side of the fish. Cut two of the oranges in half, place cut side down, then cut each half into six slices. Season the fish well, inside and out and then put a slice of orange into each incision.

2 Lightly oil a baking sheet, then arrange half the herbs over the tray. Place the fish on top, then scatter the rest of the herbs over. Drizzle with the rest of the oil.

3 Cut the remaining two oranges in half and squeeze out the juice. Pour over the fish. Bake for 25–30 minutes or until the fish is just cooked and tender.

4 Remove the herbs from the top of the fish, and cut the head off, if you wish.

5 Arrange the rocket, beetroot and almonds on four plates and place a fish on top of each. Serve with crusty bread and butter, if you like.

Baked trout with cream sauce

SERVES 4

4 whole trout, each about 250g/9oz, cleaned

50g/2oz/¼ cup butter

15ml/1 tbsp plain (all-purpose) flour

250ml/8fl oz/1 cup double (heavy) cream

100ml/3½fl oz/scant ½ cup white wine

pinch of freshly grated nutmeg

salt and ground black pepper

1 lemon, cut into wedges, and boiled new potatoes with parsley, to serve

This is a classic recipe for pan-cooked freshwater trout. The flavours of the cream, wine, nutmeg and trout complement each other beautifully.

1 Season the fish inside and out with salt. Melt the butter in a frying pan and fry the trout for 5–8 minutes, turning, until golden.

2 Stir the flour into the cream and add this to the pan. Add the wine and nutmeg, and cook, covered, for 8–10 minutes or until cooked through.

3 Serve the trout with the sauce and a wedge of lemon, with boiled new potatoes sprinkled with parsley.

COOK'S TIP The amount of sauce in this recipe makes about a ladleful for each serving. Cut down the proportions if you feel this is too much.

Trout with leek and bacon

SERVES 4

4 whole trout, each about 225g/8oz, cleaned

handful of parsley sprig

4 lemon slices

8 large leek leaves

8 bacon rashers (strips), rinds removed

salt and ground black pepper

Wrapping trout this way helps to retain moisture and adds flavour, particularly to farmed fish. If you are lucky enough to obtain wild trout, you will appreciate just how well its earthy flavour works with the bacon and leek. Make sure you use dry-cure bacon for this traditional Welsh dish.

1 Preheat the oven to 180°C/350°F/Gas 4. Rinse the trout, inside and out, under cold running water, then pat dry with kitchen paper. Season the cavities and put a few parsley sprigs and a slice of lemon into each.

2 Wrap two leek leaves, then two bacon rashers, spiral fashion around each fish. It may be helpful to secure the ends with wooden cocktail sticks or toothpicks.

3 Lay the fish in a shallow ovenproof dish, in a single layer and side by side, head next to tail.

4 Bake for about 20 minutes, until the bacon is cooked and the leeks are tender. The trout should be cooked through; check by inserting a sharp knife into the thickest part.

5 Sprinkle the remaining parsley over the trout and serve.

COOK'S TIPS This dish is nicer to eat if the backbone is removed from the fish first – you can ask your fishmonger to do this for you. Leave the head and tail on or cut them off, as you prefer.
• Use tender leaves of leek, rather than the rough outer ones. Alternatively, soften some leaves by pouring boiling water over them and leaving them to stand for a few minutes before draining.

Liquorice, walnut and fennel trout fillets

SERVES 4

4 trout fillets, each about 200g/7oz

10ml/2 tsp powdered liquorice

2.5ml/½ tsp sea salt

45–50ml/3–4 tbsp finely chopped walnuts

15ml/1 tbsp fennel seeds

20ml/4 tsp sunflower oil

lemon wedges, to garnish

steamed samphire, to serve

The aromatic flavours of liquorice and fennel are an excellent complement to the subtle-tasting trout. Fennel seeds have a slight aniseed taste and complement the powdered liquorice in this easy-to-prepare recipe. The crushed walnuts add texture to the dish. Serve hot or cold for a mid-week supper.

1 Preheat the oven to 200°C/400°F/Gas 6. Grease a large baking dish including the sides.

2 Put the trout fillets, skin-side down on the baking dish.

3 Mix together the liquorice powder, salt, chopped walnuts, fennel seeds and oil and press on to the trout, pushing down with your fingertips.

4 Bake the trout for 12–15 minutes, or until the flesh flakes easily with a fork and the topping is lightly browned. Place on four warm serving plates.

5 Serve with steamed samphire and garnish with lemon wedges.

COOK'S TIP Liquorice powder is made by steaming and pressing the roots and then grinding them down. It dissolves easily and is often used as a seasoning.

Baked trout with tomato sauce

SERVES 4

1 trout, about 1kg/2¼lb, cleaned and left whole

60ml/4 tbsp extra virgin olive oil

500ml/17fl oz/2¼ cups dry white wine

2 garlic cloves (1 left whole, and 1 crushed)

300ml/½ pint/1¼ cups passata (bottled strained tomatoes)

45ml/3 tbsp chopped parsley

salt and ground black pepper

5ml/1 tsp dried oregano, to garnish

roast potatoes, to serve

If you have a large whole trout to cook then this recipe is simplicity itself, yet still tastes fabulous. The trout is first poached in a mixture of garlic, olive oil and wine and then transformed by the addition of a rich tomato sauce.

1 Rinse the cavity of the trout and pat it dry with kitchen paper, then place in a fish kettle. Add the oil, wine, whole garlic clove, 250ml/8fl oz/1 cup cold water, and salt and pepper, then set over a high heat and bring to the boil. Reduce the heat and cook the fish very gently for 30–40 minutes.

2 Carefully lift out the fish and transfer to an shallow ovenproof serving dish.

3 Preheat the oven to 200°C/400°F/Gas 6. Put the passata into a small pan and simmer for 5 minutes with the crushed garlic, parsley, and salt and pepper to taste. Keep warm.

4 Pour the tomato sauce over the fish, and place in the oven for 2–3 minutes, until heated through. Sprinkle lightly with oregano and serve, with roast potatoes if you like.

Fried trout with Chinese wine sauce

SERVES 4

2 whole freshwater trout, each about 275g/10oz, cleaned

5ml/1 tsp salt

15ml/1 tbsp cornflour (cornstarch)

vegetable oil, for deep-frying

15ml/1 tbsp vegetable oil

4 garlic cloves, crushed

1 green (bell) pepper, thinly sliced

2 spring onions (scallions), white parts only, finely chopped

45ml/3 tbsp strong Chinese wine, such as kaoliang or rose-flavoured wine, or dry sherry

5ml/1 tsp sugar

15ml/1 tbsp sesame oil

2.5ml/½ tsp ground black pepper

Trout is an abundant fish in northern China where it is often soused with plenty of wine, ginger and pungent bean sauces. If you cannot find Chinese wine then a very dry sherry can be substituted.

1 Rub the trout with salt and rinse. Pat dry with kitchen paper, then coat with the cornflour. Heat the oil for deep-frying in a wok. Deep-fry the fish until crisp, then set aside.

2 Heat the 15ml/1 tbsp oil in a wok and fry the garlic for 2 minutes. Add the sliced green pepper and spring onions, and fry for 1 minute.

3 Add the wine or sherry, sugar, sesame oil, pepper and 200ml/ 7fl oz/scant 1 cup water, and bring to the boil. Add the trout and simmer for about 3 minutes, until the fish is cooked through and the cornflour coating has thickened the sauce.

VARIATION If you are short of time you could also use trout fillets. You will need about 400g/14oz. Trout fillets take very little time to cook so take care to watch them carefullly.

Trout fried in flour

SERVES 4

4 whole trout, each about 300g/11oz, cleaned

juice of ½ lemon, plus extra slices to garnish

30ml/2 tbsp plain (all-purpose) flour

30ml/2 tbsp sunflower oil

1kg/2¼lb potatoes

100g/3½oz butter

salt and ground white pepper

parsley and chives, chopped, to garnish

For the salad

200ml/7fl oz/1 cup natural (plain) yogurt

juice of ½ lemon

30ml/2 tbsp chopped fresh dill

1 lettuce, separated into leaves

2 tomatoes, sliced

salt, ground white pepper and pinch of sugar

By coating fish with flour and pan-frying them, you get a crispy, golden-brown crust on the outside and soft and succulent flesh on the inside. Cooking with flour is a quick and easy method of preparing fish while enhancing its taste and texture.

1 Preheat the oven to 180°C/350°F/Gas 4. Season the fish inside and out with lemon juice, salt and pepper. Spread the flour on a plate and turn the fish in it to coat. Heat the oil in a large frying pan and fry the fish carefully for 3 minutes on each side until the skin is crisp.

2 Remove the fish to a baking tray and cook in the oven for 15–20 minutes. If you can tear out the dorsal fin easily the fish is cooked. Remove the fish to a serving dish and keep warm.

3 While the fish is cooking, peel and boil the potatoes.

4 For the salad, mix the yogurt with the lemon juice and chopped dill and season with salt, pepper and sugar. Pour it over the lettuce and tomatoes and toss together.

5 Melt the butter in a small pan. Drain the potatoes and add them to the serving dish. Pour the butter over the fish and garnish with chopped parsley and chives and lemon slices. Serve immediately, with the salad.

Trout gougère

A gougère is a choux pastry ring flavoured with cheese. This one is served hot, with a creamy trout and watercress filling.

1 Preheat the oven to 200°C/400°F/Gas 6. Sift the flour on to a sheet of non-stick baking parchment. Draw a 20cm/8in circle on a separate sheet of baking parchment. Grease a baking sheet and place the parchment on it.

2 Make the choux paste for the ring. In a pan gently heat the butter and water until the butter melts. Bring to the boil then remove the pan from the heat. Quickly tip in all the sifted flour and beat the mixture with a wooden spoon until a smooth, glossy paste forms. Leave to cool for 5 minutes.

3 Add the beaten egg to the cooled paste gradually, stirring all the time to prevent the mixture from curdling. Stir in three-quarters of the grated Gruyère cheese.

4 Spoon the choux paste into a piping (pastry) bag fitted with a 1cm/½in plain round nozzle and pipe just inside the circle to form a ring. Sprinkle with the remaining cheese. Bake in the oven for 20–25 minutes or until golden brown and crisp.

5 Meanwhile, make the filling. Place the trout fillet, wine, parsley, lemon slices and bay leaf in a large frying pan. Gently poach the fish for 4–6 minutes, until it is cooked. Remove the fish from the pan. Strain the cooking liquid and reserve. Skin the fish, remove any bones and flake it into bitesize pieces.

6 Heat the butter in a pan, add the onion and fry gently for about 5 minutes until softened. Stir the flour into the pan and cook for 1 minute, stirring. Gradually add the reserved cooking liquid and the milk, stirring constantly to form a thick sauce. Add the flaked trout, cream, cheese and watercress to the sauce and season well. Heat gently until piping hot.

7 When the choux ring is cooked, remove it from the oven and place on a warmed serving plate. Slice the gougère in half horizontally and spoon in the hot trout and watercress filling. Replace the pastry lid on the ring and serve immediately.

SERVES 8–10

For the gougère
65g/2½oz/generous ½ cup plain (all-purpose) flour
50g/2oz/¼ cup butter
150ml/¼ pint/⅔ cup water
2 eggs, beaten
75g/3oz Gruyère cheese, grated
butter, for greasing

For the filling
350g/12oz trout fillets
150ml/¼ pint/⅔ cup dry white wine
4 fresh parsley sprigs
½ lemon, sliced
1 bay leaf
25g/1oz/2 tbsp butter
1 small onion, chopped
25g/1oz/¼ cup plain (all-purpose) flour
150ml/¼ pint/⅔ cup milk
60ml/4 tbsp double (heavy) cream
50g/2oz Gruyère cheese, grated
50g/2oz watercress, finely chopped
salt and ground black pepper

Trout and asparagus pie

SERVES 6–8

115g/4oz asparagus

75g/3oz/6 tbsp butter, plus extra for greasing

1 small onion, chopped

115g/4oz/1½ cups button (white) mushrooms, sliced

30ml/2 tbsp chopped fresh flat leaf parsley

250g/9oz/generous 1 cup ricotta cheese

115g/4oz/½ cup mascarpone cheese

8 filo pastry sheets, each measuring 45 x 25cm/ 18 x 10in

450g/1lb trout fillets, skinned

salt and ground black pepper

Crisp filo pastry filled with layers of trout, ricotta cheese, asparagus and mushrooms makes a dramatic-looking dish that is absurdly easy to make.

1 Preheat the oven to 200°C/400°F/Gas 6. Grease a 23cm/9in springform cake tin or pan. Bring a pan of water to the boil, add the asparagus and blanch for 3 minutes. Drain, refresh under cold water and drain again.

2 Heat 25g/1oz/2 tbsp of the butter in a frying pan and add the onion. Cook for 3–5 minutes or until softened. Add the mushrooms and cook for 2 minutes more. Stir in the parsley and season well with salt and black pepper.

3 In a mixing bowl combine the ricotta and mascarpone cheeses. Stir in the onion mixture. Melt the remaining butter in a small pan.

4 Line the cake tin with the filo pastry sheets, brushing each layer with melted butter and leaving the edges hanging over the sides of the tin. While you are working with one filo pastry sheet, keep the rest covered with a damp, clean dishtowel so that they do not dry out.

5 Place half the ricotta mixture in the base of the filo-lined tin. Remove any remaining pin bones from the trout fillets, then arrange them in a single layer over the ricotta. Season well.

6 Top with the asparagus and the remaining ricotta mixture. Bring the overhanging edges of the pastry over the top, and brush the layers with the remaining butter.

7 Bake the pie for 25 minutes or until golden brown. Cover loosely with foil and cook for a further 15 minutes.

8 Remove the pie from the tin and place it on a warmed serving plate. Serve in slices.

GRAINS, NOODLES AND PASTA

You don't need a lot of trout to make an impact in a rice or pasta dish. In Trout and Prosciutto Risotto Rolls, for instance, there is just one trout fillet per person, but when that fillet is curled around a delectable prawn and risotto mixture the results are superb. Trout is very good in pasta dishes, too, whether cold, as in Smoked Trout Pasta Salad, or hot, as in Malaysian Steamed Trout with Noodles.

Trout with black rice

SERVES 2

2.5cm/1in piece fresh root ginger, peeled and grated

1 garlic clove, crushed

1 fresh red chilli, seeded and finely chopped

30ml/2 tbsp soy sauce

2 trout fillets, each about 225g/8oz

oil, for greasing

For the rice

15ml/1 tbsp sesame oil

50g/2oz/¾ cup fresh shiitake mushrooms, sliced

8 spring onions (scallions), finely chopped

150g/5oz/¾ cup black rice

4 slices fresh root ginger

900ml/1½ pints/3¾ cups boiling water

Pink trout fillets cooked with ginger, garlic and chilli make a stunning contrast to the nutty black rice.

1 Make the rice. Heat the sesame oil in a pan and fry the mushrooms with half the spring onions for 2–3 minutes.

2 Add the rice and sliced ginger to the pan and stir well. Cover with the boiling water and bring to the boil. Reduce the heat, cover and simmer for 25–30 minutes or until the rice is tender. Drain well and cover to keep warm.

3 While the rice is cooking, preheat the oven to 200°C/400°F/ Gas 6. In a small bowl mix together the grated ginger, garlic, chilli and soy sauce.

4 Place the fish, skin-side up, in a lightly oiled shallow baking dish. Using a sharp knife, make several slits in the skin of the fish, then spread the ginger paste all over the fillets.

5 Cover the dish tightly with foil and cook in the oven for 20–25 minutes or until the trout fillets are cooked through.

6 Divide the rice between two warmed serving plates. Remove the ginger. Lay the fish on top and sprinkle over the reserved spring onions.

Smoked trout risotto

The rich flavours of smoked trout permeate this simple risotto. The most important point to remember when you're making risotto is that you need to be patient. The rice needs constant stirring and once all the liquid has been absorbed it is best served straight away.

1 For the creamiest risotto the stock needs to be hot when it is added to the rice, so keep it simmering in a pan.

2 Heat the oil in a large pan. Add the chopped onion and fry it gently over a low heat for about 5 minutes until softened. Do not allow the onion to brown.

3 Add the rice to the pan and stir well with a wooden spoon to coat each grain thoroughly in oil. Cook over a low heat for 2–3 minutes until the rice grains have turned translucent.

4 Pour the white wine over the rice in the pan, stirring constantly. Continue to stir for 1–2 minutes until all of the wine has been absorbed.

5 Keeping the pan over a medium heat, add the hot stock, a ladleful at a time, stirring all the time.

6 Add another ladleful of stock to the rice only when the previous quantity has been absorbed, and continue in this way until all the stock has been used up. This will take around 20 minutes. As the rice cooks the mixture will thicken – the risotto is cooked when the rice has a velvety texture.

7 Remove the pan from the heat and stir in the crème fraîche or sour cream and the grated Parmesan cheese. Add three-quarters of the chopped smoked trout and the chopped chervil. Season and stir well to mix. Cover the pan and leave to stand for about 2 minutes.

8 Divide the risotto among four warmed serving plates, top with the remaining smoked trout and garnish with the fresh chervil sprigs. Extra grated Parmesan cheese can be offered separately.

SERVES 4

1.2 litres/2 pints/5 cups simmering fish stock

30ml/2 tbsp olive oil

1 medium onion, finely chopped

400g/14oz/2 cups risotto rice, preferably arborio

150ml/¼ pint/⅔ cup dry white wine

45ml/3 tbsp crème fraîche or sour cream

45ml/3 tbsp grated Parmesan cheese, plus extra to serve

350g/12oz smoked trout, roughly chopped

60ml/4 tbsp chopped fresh chervil, plus extra sprigs to garnish

salt and ground black pepper

Spicy trout risotto

Lovely and creamy, this trout risotto rings the changes with warming spices to add a twist to the dish. Make sure the trout is really fresh for the best results and that the spices have not lost any of their pungency.

1 Put the bay leaf, spices and two-thirds of the chopped parsley into a pan large enough to take the fish, and cover with water. Simmer gently for 10 minutes, then lower the trout into the water.

2 Poach for 5 minutes, then cover and remove from the heat. Leave the trout in the hot water until cooked through. The cooking time needed will depend on the size of each fish.

3 Remove the trout, then skin and fillet them. Strain the stock into a pan. Bring to the boil then reduce the heat to a simmer.

4 Heat half the butter and the oil in a heavy pan, add the garlic and cook until just softened. Add the rice and toast the grains well, then add the wine and cook for 2 minutes.

5 Add one ladleful of hot fish stock and cook, stirring constantly, until the liquid is absorbed. Continue in this way, adding the stock a ladleful at a time and stirring constantly. Always allow the liquid to be absorbed before adding more.

6 After the rice has been cooking for about 20 minutes, stir in the fish fillets, breaking them up as you stir them through.

7 When the rice is tender, remove the pan from the heat and stir in the remaining butter. Season to taste.

8 Cover and leave to rest for 2 minutes, then transfer to a platter. Sprinkle with the remaining chopped parsley and serve immediately.

SERVES 2

1 bay leaf

5 black peppercorns

½ cinnamon stick

2 cloves

pinch of freshly grated nutmeg

pinch of ground ginger

pinch of ground allspice

90ml/6 tbsp chopped fresh flat leaf parsley

2 or 3 whole trout, each about 225g/8oz, cleaned

75g/3oz/6 tbsp unsalted butter

30ml/2 tbsp olive oil

1 garlic clove, chopped

350g/12oz risotto rice, preferably arborio

175ml/6fl oz/¾ cup dry white wine

salt and ground black pepper

Trout and prosciutto risotto rolls

This makes a delicious and elegant meal. The risotto – made with porcini mushrooms and prawns – is a fine match for the robust flavour of the trout rolls.

1 First make the risotto. Heat the oil in a large, heavy saucepan or deep frying pan and fry the prawns very briefly until flecked with pink. Lift out with a slotted spoon and transfer to a plate.

2 Add the chopped onion to the oil remaining in the pan and fry over a gentle heat for 3–4 minutes until soft. Add the rice and stir for 3–4 minutes until the grains are evenly coated in oil. Add 75ml/5 tbsp of the wine and then the stock, a little at a time, stirring over a gentle heat and allowing the rice to absorb the liquid before adding more.

SERVES 4

---

4 trout fillets, each about 225g/8oz, skinned

4 slices prosciutto

capers, to garnish

For the risotto

30ml/2 tbsp olive oil

8 large peeled raw prawns (shrimp)

1 medium onion, chopped

225g/8oz/generous 1 cup risotto rice

about 105ml/7 tbsp white wine

about 750ml/1¼ pints/3 cups simmering fish stock

15g/½oz/2 tbsp dried porcini or chanterelle mushrooms, soaked for 10 minutes in warm water to cover

salt and ground black pepper

3 Strain the mushrooms, reserving the liquid, and cut the larger ones in half. Towards the end of cooking, stir the mushrooms into the risotto with 15ml/1 tbsp of the reserved mushroom liquid. The rice should be soft and creamy, with just a little "bite" in the centre of the grain. If necessary, add a little more stock or mushroom liquid and cook for a few minutes more. Season to taste with salt and pepper.

4 Remove the pan from the heat and stir in the prawns. Preheat the oven to 190°C/375°F/Gas 5.

5 Take a trout fillet, place a spoonful of risotto at one end and roll up. Wrap each fillet in a slice of prosciutto and place in a greased baking dish.

6 Spoon any remaining risotto around the fish fillets and sprinkle over the rest of the wine. Cover loosely with foil and bake for 15–20 minutes until the fish is tender. Spoon the risotto on to a platter, top with the trout rolls and garnish with capers. Serve immediately.

Trout with rice, tomatoes and nuts

SERVES 4

2 whole trout, each about 500g/1¼lb, cleaned

75g/3oz/¾ cup mixed unsalted cashew nuts, pine nuts, almonds and hazelnuts

25ml/1½ tbsp olive oil, plus extra for drizzling

1 small onion, finely chopped

10ml/2 tsp grated fresh root ginger

175g/6oz/1½ cups cooked white long grain rice

4 tomatoes, peeled and very finely chopped

4 sun-dried tomatoes in oil, drained and chopped

30ml/2 tbsp chopped fresh tarragon, plus extra sprigs

salt and ground black pepper

dressed green leaves, to serve

This recipe comes from northern Spain, where trout is very popular. If you fillet the fish before you bake it, it cooks more evenly and no bones get in the way of the stuffing.

1 Using a sharp knife, fillet the trout. Check the cavity for any remaining tiny bones and remove these with tweezers.

2 Preheat the oven to 190°C/375°F/Gas 5. Spread out the nuts in a baking tray and bake for 3–4 minutes, shaking the tray occasionally. Chop the nuts.

3 Heat the oil in a small frying pan and fry the onion for 3–4 minutes until soft. Stir in the ginger, cook for 1 minute more, then spoon into a mixing bowl.

4 Add the rice to the mixture in the bowl, then stir in the tomatoes, sun-dried tomatoes, toasted nuts and tarragon. Season the stuffing with plenty of salt and black pepper.

5 Place each of the trout in turn on a large piece of oiled foil and spoon the stuffing into the cavity. Add a sprig of tarragon and a drizzle of olive oil.

6 Fold the foil over to enclose each trout and put the parcels in a large roasting pan. Bake for 20–25 minutes until the fish is tender. Cut the fish into thick slices. Serve with dressed green salad leaves.

Quinoa-stuffed trout

SERVES 4

30ml/2 tbsp olive oil

1 medium onion, finely diced

1 clove garlic, crushed

30ml/2 tbsp sumac

2.5ml/½ tsp ground cinnamon

550ml/18fl oz/2½ cups fish stock

juice and rind of 1 lemon, plus finely cut lemon rind shreds, to garnish

175g/6oz/1 cup pearl quinoa

50g/2oz/⅓ cup finely chopped dried apricots

50g/2oz/⅓ cup raisins

4 whole trout, each about 225g/8oz, cleaned

salt and ground black pepper

roasted potatoes and watercress leaves, to serve

Sumac comes from the berries of a shrub that grows in Africa and North America. It has a rich red colour and adds a lovely tangy flavour to food. Here, it offsets the rich oiliness of trout, which is stuffed with quinoa, dried fruit and herbs. This dish looks impressive but is deceptively easy to make. Serve any leftover stuffing with the fish and roasted potatoes.

1 Heat the oven to 180°C/350°F/Gas 4. Heat 15ml/1 tbsp of the olive oil in a pan and add the onion, garlic, sumac and cinnamon.

2 Fry for a few minutes to soften the onion and release the spice flavours. Add the stock to the pan with the lemon juice and rind, and stir in the quinoa.

3 Bring to the boil and simmer for 8 minutes. Add the apricots and raisins, and simmer for a further few minutes until the quinoa is cooked and the fruit plump. Season to taste.

4 Pat the fish dry with kitchen paper. Brush the skin with the remaining oil and lay the whole fish on a board to enable stuffing. Fill each fish with the fruited quinoa mix. Place the fish in a serving dish and cover with foil.

5 Bake for 20–30 minutes, until the fish is light pink and flaky. Dry-fry leftover stuffing in a frying pan to reheat.

6 Garnish the fish with lemon rind shreds and serve with the reheated stuffing, roasted potatoes and watercress.

Malaysian steamed trout with noodles

SERVES 4

8 trout fillets, each about 115g/4oz, skinned

45ml/3 tbsp grated creamed coconut or desiccated (dry unsweetened shredded) coconut

grated rind and juice of 2 limes, plus extra slices to garnish

45ml/3 tbsp chopped fresh coriander (cilantro), plus extra to garnish

15ml/1 tbsp groundnut (peanut) oil

2.5–5ml/½–1 tsp chilli oil

350g/12oz broad egg noodles

salt and ground black pepper

This simple dish, served on a bed of noodles, can be prepared extremely quickly. It is suitable for any fish fillets.

1 Cut four rectangles of baking parchment, each twice the size of the trout fillets. Place a fillet on each piece and season.

2 Mix together the coconut, lime rind and chopped coriander and spread one-quarter of the mixture over each trout fillet. Sandwich another trout fillet on top.

3 Mix the lime juice with the oils, adjusting the quantity of chilli oil to your own taste, and drizzle the mixture over the trout 'sandwiches'.

4 Prepare a steamer. Fold up the edges of the paper and pleat them over the trout to make parcels, making sure they are well sealed.

5 Place in the steamer basket and steam over the simmering water for about 10–15 minutes, depending on the thickness of the trout fillets.

6 Meanwhile, cook the noodles in a large pan of boiling water for 5–8 minutes, until just tender. Drain, toss with a little chilli oil, if you like, and divide among four warmed plates. Remove each trout 'sandwich' from its wrapper and place on top of the noodles. Garnish with the lime slices and coriander.

Fusilli with smoked trout

SERVES 4

2 carrots, cut into matchsticks

1 leek, cut into matchsticks

2 celery sticks, cut into matchsticks

150ml/¼ pint/⅔ cup vegetable stock

225g/8oz smoked trout fillets, skinned and cut into strips

200g/7oz cream cheese

150ml/¼ pint/⅔ cup medium sweet white wine or fish stock

15ml/1 tbsp chopped fresh dill or fennel

225g/8oz/2 cups long curly fusilli or other dried pasta shapes

salt and ground black pepper

In its creamy sauce, the smoked trout blends beautifully with the still crisp-tender vegetables in this classic pasta dish.

1 Put the carrot, leek and celery matchsticks into a pan and add the stock. Bring to the boil and cook quickly for 4–5 minutes, until most of the stock has evaporated. Remove from the heat and add the smoked trout.

2 Put the cream cheese and wine or fish stock into a pan over a medium heat, and whisk until smooth. Add the dill or fennel and season.

3 Cook the fusilli in a pan of salted boiling water according to the instructions on the packet. When the pasta is tender, but still firm to the bite, drain, and return it to the pan.

4 Add the sauce, toss lightly and transfer to a serving bowl. Top with the cooked vegetables and trout. Serve immediately.

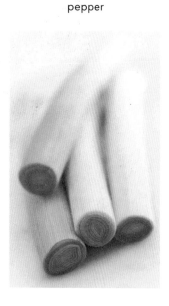

Spicy trout cannelloni

One of the most popular pasta dishes, cannelloni usually has a meat and tomato filling, or one based on spinach and ricotta cheese. Smoked trout makes a delicious change in this low-fat version.

1 Put the onion, garlic clove and stock in a large pan. Cover and simmer for 3 minutes. Remove the lid and cook until the stock has reduced entirely.

2 Stir in the tomatoes and dried herbs. Simmer uncovered for 10 minutes, or until the mixture is very thick.

3 Skin the trout with a sharp knife. Flake the flesh, discarding any bones. Put the fish in a bowl and add the tomato mixture, peas and breadcrumbs. Mix well, then season to taste.

4 Spoon the filling generously into the cannelloni tubes and arrange them in an ovenproof dish. Preheat the oven to 190°C/375°F/Gas 5.

5 Make the sauce. Put the butter, flour and milk into a pan and cook over a medium heat, whisking constantly, until the sauce boils and thickens. Simmer for 2–3 minutes, stirring all the time. Season to taste with salt, freshly ground black pepper and grated nutmeg.

6 Pour the sauce over the stuffed cannelloni and sprinkle with the grated Parmesan cheese. Bake for 30–45 minutes, or until the top is golden and bubbling. Serve immediately.

SERVES 4–6

1 large onion, finely chopped

1 garlic clove, crushed

60ml/4 tbsp vegetable stock

2 x 400g/14oz cans chopped tomatoes

2.5ml/½ tsp dried mixed herbs

225g/8oz smoked trout fillets

75g/3oz/½ cup frozen peas, thawed

75g/3oz/1½ cups fresh breadcrumbs

16 pre-cooked cannelloni tubes

salt and ground black pepper

For the sauce

25g/1oz/2 tbsp butter

25g/1oz/¼ cup plain (all-purpose) flour

350ml/12fl oz/1½ cups skimmed milk

freshly grated nutmeg

25ml/1½ tbsp freshly grated Parmesan cheese

Smoked trout pasta salad

SERVES 4

15g/½oz/1 tbsp butter

1 bulb fennel, finely chopped

6 spring onions (scallions), 2 very finely chopped and 4 thinly sliced

225g/8oz smoked trout fillets, skinned and flaked

45ml/3 tbsp chopped fresh dill

120ml/4fl oz/½ cup mayonnaise

10ml/2 tsp lemon juice

30ml/2 tbsp whipping cream

450g/1lb small pasta shapes, such as shells

salt and ground black pepper

fresh dill sprigs, to garnish

Choose hollow pasta shapes, such as shells or penne, which trap the creamy filling, creating tasty mouthfuls of trout, fennel and spring onion. The addition of dill is not only attractive, but also gives this salad a distinctive flavour.

1 Melt the butter in a small frying pan. Add the fennel and finely chopped spring onions and fry over a medium heat for 3–5 minutes. Transfer to a large bowl and leave to cool slightly.

2 Add the sliced spring onions, trout, dill, mayonnaise, lemon juice and cream to the bowl with the fennel. Season lightly with salt and pepper and mix gently until well blended.

3 Bring a large pan of lightly salted water to the boil. Add the pasta. Cook according to the instructions on the packet until al dente. Drain thoroughly in a colander and leave to cool.

4 Add the pasta to the vegetable and trout mixture and toss to coat evenly. Taste for seasoning. Serve the salad lightly chilled or at room temperature, garnished with sprigs of dill.

ON THE GRILL

Anglers swear the best place to eat trout is in the open air, and if these superb recipes are anything to go by, they are probably right. As the sun goes down, sit on the patio and tuck into Hot and Fragrant Trout, Cheese-topped Trout, or Trout in Wine Sauce with Plantain. Kids will love the Trout Burgers, so be sure to prepare plenty.

Trout burgers

These home-made fish burgers really are a treat. They provide the ideal way of persuading children who claim they don't like fish to try it. Cook chilled burgers on the barbecue, or, if you prefer, on a lightly oiled grill rack.

1 Place the trout in a frying pan with the milk, stock and spring onions. Simmer for 5 minutes or until the fish is cooked. Lift it out of the pan and set it aside. Strain the stock through a sieve into a bowl, reserving the spring onions until required.

2 Mash the potatoes roughly and stir in the tartare sauce, egg and breadcrumbs. Flake the trout and add the reserved spring onions. Fold into the potato mixture and season

3 Divide the potato mixture into eight and shape into burgers, using your hands. Coat thoroughly in the semolina and pat them into shape. Arrange on a plate and place in the refrigerator for 1 hour, so that they firm up.

4 In a bowl, mix the mayonnaise with the corn kernels and diced red pepper.

5 Heat the oil in a frying pan and fry the burgers for 10 minutes, turning once.

6 To serve, split open the buns and spread a little of the mayonnaise over the bottom half. Fill with a few salad leaves, a couple of tomato slices and a fish burger. Serve immediately.

COOK'S TIP Not all children like tartare sauce. If you have any doubts about adding it to the burger mixture, you could substitute tomato ketchup instead.

MAKES 8

350g/12oz trout fillets, skinned

150ml/¼ pint/⅔ cup milk

150ml/¼ pint/⅔ cup hot fish stock

4 spring onions (scallions), thinly sliced

350g/12oz cooked potatoes, peeled

5ml/1 tsp tartare sauce

1 egg, beaten

50g/2oz/1 cup fresh white breadcrumbs

60ml/4 tbsp semolina

salt and ground white pepper

vegetable oil, for shallow frying

To serve

120ml/4fl oz/½ cup mayonnaise

45ml/3 tbsp drained canned whole kernel corn

1 red (bell) pepper, seeded and finely diced

8 burger buns

4 ripe tomatoes, sliced

salad leaves

Cheese-topped trout

SERVES 4

50g/2oz/1 cup fresh white breadcrumbs

50g/2oz Parmesan cheese, finely grated

25g/1oz/⅓ cup pine nuts, chopped

15ml/1 tbsp chopped fresh parsley

15ml/1 tbsp chopped fresh coriander (cilantro)

30ml/2 tbsp olive oil

4 thick trout fillets, each about 225g/8oz

40g/1½oz/3 tbsp butter

juice of 1 lemon

salt and ground black pepper

lemon slices, to garnish

steamed baby asparagus and carrots, to serve

For this simple yet sophisticated supper dish, succulent strips of filleted trout are topped with a mixture of Parmesan cheese, pine nuts, herbs and breadcrumbs before being drizzled with lemon butter and grilled until tender.

1 In a mixing bowl, combine the breadcrumbs, Parmesan cheese, pine nuts, parsley and coriander. Add the oil.

2 Cut each trout fillet into two strips. Firmly press the breadcrumb mixture on to the top of each strip of trout.

3 Preheat the grill or broiler to high. Grease the grill pan with 15g/½oz of the butter. Melt the remaining butter in a small pan and stir in the lemon juice. Season with a little salt and black pepper.

4 Place the breadcrumb-topped fillets on the greased grill pan and pour the lemon butter over.

5 Grill or broil the trout for 10 minutes or until the fillets are just cooked. Place two trout strips on each plate, garnish with lemon slices and serve with steamed asparagus and carrots.

Hot and fragrant trout

SERVES 4

2 large fresh green chillies, seeded and roughly chopped

5 shallots, peeled

5 garlic cloves, peeled

30ml/2 tbsp fresh lime juice

30ml/2 tbsp Thai fish sauce

15ml/1 tbsp palm sugar or light muscovado (molasses) sugar

4 kaffir lime leaves, rolled into cigarette shapes and finely sliced

2 whole trout, each about 350g/12oz, cleaned

Chinese chives, to garnish

boiled rice, to serve

This wickedly hot marinade could be used with any firm-fleshed fish or meat. It also makes a wonderful spicy dip for grilled or barbecued meat.

1 Wrap the green chillies, shallots and garlic cloves in a foil package. Place under a hot grill or broiler for 10 minutes, until the vegetables have softened.

2 As soon as the foil package is cool enough to handle, unwrap it and tip the contents into a mortar or food processor. Blend to a paste. Add the lime juice, fish sauce, sugar and lime leaves and mix well.

3 With a teaspoon, stuff this paste inside the fish. Smear a little on the skin too. Grill or broil the fish for about 5 minutes on each side, until just cooked through.

4 Carefully lift the fish on to a platter. Serve with rice, garnished with Chinese chives.

COOK'S TIPS Thai fish sauce (nam pla) is made from anchovies, which are salted, and then fermented in wooden barrels. The sauce, which is ubiquitous in Thai cooking, accentuates the flavour of food.
• Kaffir lime leaves release a distinctive lemony flavour when roughly chopped or torn. They are obtainable in Asian food stores. They will keep for several days, or can be frozen.

Trout in wine sauce with barbecued plantain

In the West Indies, where this recipe originated, the fish used would probably be dolphinfish or snapper, but this is also a wonderful treatment for trout.

1 Put the trout fillets in a dish. Mix the garlic, pepper, paprika, celery salt, curry powder and sugar in a bowl. Sprinkle over the trout and marinate for 1 hour.

2 Melt the butter in a large frying pan and sauté the marinated trout fillets, in batches if necessary, for about 5 minutes or until cooked through, turning once. Transfer to a warm plate and keep hot.

3 Add the wine, fish stock and honey to the pan. Bring to the boil and simmer to reduce slightly. Return the fillets to the pan and spoon over the sauce. Sprinkle with parsley and simmer gently for a few minutes.

4 Meanwhile, prepare the barbecue. Position a grill rack over the coals to heat. Wrap the plantain in foil and when the coals are medium-hot, bake on the barbecue for about 10 minutes, or until tender, before cutting it into rounds.

5 Transfer the fish to warmed serving plates, stir the sauce and pour it over. Garnish with the baked plantain and lime wedges.

SERVES 4–6

4 trout fillets, each about 225g/8oz, skinned
15ml/1 tbsp crushed garlic
7.5ml/1½ tsp coarse-grain black pepper
7.5ml/1½ tsp paprika
7.5ml/1½ tsp celery salt
7.5ml/1½ tsp curry powder
5ml/1 tsp caster (superfine) sugar
25g/1oz/2 tbsp butter
150ml/¼ pint/⅔cup white wine
150ml/¼ pint/⅔ cup fish stock
10ml/2 tsp clear honey
15–30ml/1–2 tbsp chopped fresh parsley
1 yellow plantain
oil, for frying
lime wedges, to garnish

Spicy barbecued sea trout

SERVES 4

6 sea trout cutlets, each about 115g/4oz

2 garlic cloves, chopped

1 fresh long red chilli, seeded and chopped

45ml/3 tbsp chopped Thai basil

15ml/1 tbsp palm sugar or granulated sugar

3 limes

400ml/14fl oz/1²/₃ cups coconut milk

15ml/1 tbsp Thai fish sauce

Sea trout has a superb texture and a flavour like that of wild salmon. It is best served with strong but complementary flavours, such as chillies and lime, that cut the richness of its flesh.

1 Place the sea trout cutlets side by side in a shallow dish. Using a pestle, pound the garlic and chilli in a large mortar to break both up roughly. Add 30ml/2 tbsp of the Thai basil with the sugar and continue to pound to a rough paste.

2 Grate the rind from 1 lime and squeeze it. Mix the rind and juice into the chilli paste, with the coconut milk. Pour the mixture over the cutlets. Cover and chill for about 1 hour. Cut the remaining limes into wedges.

3 Take the fish out of the refrigerator so that it can return to room temperature.

4 Prepare the barbecue. When the coals are medium-hot remove the cutlets from the marinade and place them in an oiled hinged wire fish basket or directly on the lightly oiled grill. Cook the fish for 4 minutes on each side, trying not to move them. They may stick to the grill rack if not seared first.

5 Strain the remaining marinade into a pan, reserving the contents of the sieve. Bring the marinade to the boil, then simmer gently for 5 minutes, stirring. Stir in the contents of the sieve and continue to simmer for 1 minute more. Add the Thai fish sauce and the remaining Thai basil.

6 Lift each fish cutlet on to a plate, pour over the sauce and serve with the lime wedges.

COOK'S TIP Sea trout is best cooked when the barbecue is cool to medium hot, and the coals have a medium to thick coating of ash. Always remember to oil the barbecue rack of a hinged grill lightly and take care when cooking any fish in a marinade, as the residue can cause flare-ups if it drips on to the coals.

Bacon-wrapped trout with oatmeal

This stuffing is based on a Scottish speciality called Skirlie, which is a mixture of oatmeal and onion. This trout can also be baked in the oven if preferred.

1 Chop two of the bacon rashers. Melt 25g/1oz/2 tbsp of the butter or bacon fat in a large frying pan and cook the chopped bacon briefly. Add the finely chopped onion and fry gently for 5–8 minutes, until softened.

2 Add the oatmeal and cook until the oatmeal darkens and absorbs the fat, but do not allow it to overbrown. Stir in the parsley and chives, with salt and pepper to taste. Cool.

3 Wash and dry the trout, then stuff with the oatmeal mixture. Wrap each fish in two bacon rashers, dot with the remaining butter and sprinkle with the lemon juice. Place the fish in an oiled hinged wire fish basket.

4 Prepare the barbecue. When the coals are medium-hot cook the fish on the barbecue for 4 minutes each side.

5 Meanwhile, make the mayonnaise. Place the watercress, chives and parsley in a sieve and pour boiling water over them. Drain, rinse under cold water, and drain well on kitchen paper.

6 Purée the herbs in a mortar with a pestle. (This is easier than using a food processor for a quantity as small as this.) Stir the puréed herbs into the lemon mayonnaise with the fromage frais, crème fraîche or sour cream. Add tarragon mustard to taste and stir well.

7 When cooked, transfer the trout to warmed serving plates. Serve with watercress, cherry tomatoes and lemon wedges, accompanied by the herb mayonnaise.

SERVES 4

10 dry-cured streaky (fatty) bacon rashers

40g/1½oz/3 tbsp butter or bacon fat

1 onion, finely chopped

115g/4oz/1 cup oatmeal

30ml/2 tbsp chopped fresh parsley

30ml/2 tbsp chopped fresh chives

4 whole trout, each about 350g/12oz, cleaned and boned

juice of ½ lemon

salt and ground black pepper

watercress, cherry tomatoes and lemon wedges, to serve

For the herb mayonnaise

6 watercress sprigs

15ml/1 tbsp chopped fresh chives

30ml/2 tbsp roughly chopped fresh parsley

90ml/6 tbsp lemon mayonnaise

30ml/2 tbsp fromage frais, crème fraîche or sour cream

2.5–5ml/½–1 tsp tarragon mustard

Stuffed grilled trout

SERVES 4–6

2 whole trout, each about
500g/1¼ lb, cleaned

120ml/8 tbsp soft breadcrumbs

juice of 1 lemon

150ml/10 tbsp extra virgin
olive oil, plus extra for
brushing

30ml/2 tbsp chopped fresh
flat leaf parsley

salt and ground
black pepper

This is a very simple but fabulous way of serving trout. A fresh breadcrumb, lemon juice, olive oil and parsley stuffing complements the oily flesh of the grilled trout beautifully.

1 Light the barbecue and wait until you have a heap of hot, even red embers. Position the grill rack. Rinse the trout under cold running water inside and out. Pat dry with kitchen paper.

2 In a small bowl, mix the breadcrumbs with the lemon juice, half the olive oil and the parsley and season to taste with salt and pepper.

3 Stuff the inside of each trout with this mixture. Score each trout lightly on each side through the skin, and rub the remaining oil all over the fish.

4 Lay the fish on an oiled grill rack and cook for about 10 minutes on each side, until the trout is cooked through, brushing with more oil during the cooking process.

Trout with curried orange butter

Trout are perfect for a midweek meal, especially served with this delicious tangy butter. Children will love the buttery curry flavour but it would be better to fillet the cooked trout to remove the bone before giving this to young children.

1 Mix the softened butter, curry powder, rosemary and orange rind together in a bowl with salt and plenty of ground black pepper. Wrap in foil and freeze for 10 minutes.

2 Brush the fish all over with oil and sprinkle well with seasoning. Make three diagonal slashes through the skin and flesh on each side of the fish.

3 Cut the flavoured butter into small pieces and carefully insert into the slashes made in the fish.

4 Thread the orange halves onto metal skewers.

5 Place the orange halves and fish on the grill or broiling pan and cook under a preheated high grill or broiler or hot barbecue for 3–4 minutes on each side, depending on the thickness of the fish. Garnish with wedges of grilled orange before serving with boiled new potatoes.

SERVES 3–4

25g/1oz/2 tbsp butter,
softened

5ml/1 tsp curry powder

3 sprigs rosemary, torn

5ml/1 tsp grated orange rind

4 whole trout, each about
225g/8oz, cleaned and
heads removed

vegetable or sunflower oil,
for brushing

salt and ground black
pepper

4 oranges, cut in half,
to garnish

boiled new potatoes,
to serve

Nutritional notes

The nutritional analysis given for each recipe is calculated per portion (i.e. serving or item), unless otherwise stated. If the recipe gives a range, such as Serves 4–6, then the nutritional analysis will be for the smaller portion size, i.e. 6 servings. The analysis does not include optional ingredients, such as salt added to taste.

Trout bisque: Energy 355kcal/1475kJ; Protein 14g; Carbohydrate 14g, of which sugars 7g; Fat 27g, of which saturates 14g; Cholesterol 89mg; Calcium 50mg; Fibre 2g; Sodium 192mg.

Smoked trout cocottes: Energy 426kcal/1762kJ; Protein 16.8g; Carbohydrate 12.4g, of which sugars 11.7g; Fat 34.6g, of which saturates 16.3g; Cholesterol 74mg; Calcium 175mg; Fibre 3.7g; Sodium 816mg.

Sea trout mousse: Energy 241kcal/999kJ; Protein 12.3g; Carbohydrate 1.8g, of which sugars 1.8g; Fat 20g, of which saturates 14.5g; Cholesterol 9mg; Calcium 104mg; Fibre 0.1g; Sodium 127mg.

Trout and prawn pots: Energy 183kcal/757kJ; Protein 12.2g; Carbohydrate 1.5g, of which sugars 1.3g; Fat 14.3g, of which saturates 7g; Cholesterol 107mg; Calcium 108mg; Fibre 0.5g; Sodium 207mg.

Three fish mousse: Energy 334kcal/1386kJ; Protein 25g; Carbohydrate 2g, of which sugars 2g; Fat 25g, of which saturates 14g; Cholesterol 161mg; Calcium 101mg; Fibre 0g; Sodium 506mg.

Smoked trout terrine: (per slice) Energy 348kcal/1437kJ; Protein 13.2g; Carbohydrate 1.9g, of which sugars 1.8g; Fat 32g, of which saturates 18.6g; Cholesterol 76mg; Calcium 38mg; Fibre 0.3g; Sodium 47mg.

Tea-smoked trout: Energy 357kcal/1486kJ; Protein 34.6g; Carbohydrate 3.5g, of which sugars 1.3g; Fat 24.7g, of which saturates 3.1g; Cholesterol 44mg; Calcium 119mg; Fibre 0g; Sodium 2357mg.

Trout gravadlax: Energy 314kcal/1320kJ; Protein 49.2g; Carbohydrate 0.1g, of which sugars 0.1g; Fat 13.1g, of which saturates 2.8g; Cholesterol 168mg; Calcium 63mg; Fibre 0.2g; Sodium 1588mg.

Spiced trout salad: Energy 437kcal/1834kJ; Protein 26g; Carbohydrate 37g, of which sugars 3g; Fat 22g, of which saturates 4g; Cholesterol 75mg; Calcium 41mg; Fibre 3g; Sodium 574mg.

Smoked trout salad: Energy 71kcal/294kJ; Protein 2g; Carbohydrate 6g, of which sugars 1g; Fat 5g, of which saturates 1g; Cholesterol 6mg; Calcium 13mg; Fibre 1g; Sodium 29mg.

Smoked trout tartlets: Energy 469kcal/1953kJ; Protein 17g; Carbohydrate 25g, of which sugars 4g; Fat 33g, of which saturates 21g; Cholesterol 94mg; Calcium 298mg; Fibre 0g; Sodium 515mg.

Seared trout bruschetta: Energy 473kcal/2001kJ; Protein 22.6g; Carbohydrate 68g, of which sugars 4g; Fat 14.2g, of which saturates 5.5g; Cholesterol 56mg; Calcium 176mg; Fibre 4.2g; Sodium 789mg.

Hot trout sandwich: Energy 487kcal/2033kJ; Protein 29g; Carbohydrate 26g, of which sugars 26g; Fat 30g, of which saturates 5g; Cholesterol 84mg; Calcium 106mg; Fibre 2g; Sodium 313mg.

Goat's cheese and trout toasties: Energy 349kcal/1467kJ; Protein 13g; Carbohydrate 41g, of which sugars 3g; Fat 16g, of which saturates 4g; Cholesterol 22mg; Calcium 249mg; Fibre 3g; Sodium 629mg.

Cheese scones with trout butter: Energy 473kcal/2001kJ; Protein 22.6g; Carbohydrate 68g, of which sugars 4g; Fat 14.2g, of which saturates 5.5g; Cholesterol 56mg; Calcium 176mg; Fibre 4.2g; Sodium 789mg.

Smoked trout soufflé omelette: Energy 753kcal/3126kJ; Protein 41.4g; Carbohydrate 8.7g, of which sugars 8.6g; Fat 61.7g, of which saturates 27.3g; Cholesterol 573mg; Calcium 540mg; Fibre 5.3g; Sodium 1560mg.

Trout-filled pittas with mustard mayo: Energy 603kcal/2517kJ; Protein 20.3g; Carbohydrate 46.5g, of which sugars 6.6g; Fat 38.6g, of which saturates 5.6g; Cholesterol 47mg; Calcium 144mg; Fibre 3.4g; Sodium 1524mg.

Baked trout with a gremolata crust: Energy 237kcal/992kJ; Protein 20g; Carbohydrate 12g, of which sugars 7g; Fat 13g, of which saturates 2g; Cholesterol 59mg; Calcium 43mg; Fibre 3g; Sodium 92mg.

Chinese-style steamed trout: Energy 427kcal/1788kJ; Protein 53g; Carbohydrate 2g, of which sugars 1g; Fat 23g, of which saturates 4g; Cholesterol 179mg; Calcium 57mg; Fibre 1g; Sodium 226mg.

Trout with tamarind and chilli sauce: Energy 352kcal/1481kJ; Protein 55g; Carbohydrate 3.3g, of which sugars 2.8g; Fat 13.4g, of which saturates 2.8g; Cholesterol 224mg; Calcium 95mg; Fibre 0.4g; Sodium 721mg.

Smoked trout with horseradish sauce: Energy 134kcal/561kJ; Protein 19.5g; Carbohydrate 3.1g, of which sugars 2.7g; Fat 4.9g, of which saturates 0.3g; Cholesterol 30mg; Calcium 89mg; Fibre 1.4g; Sodium 413mg.

Trout baked in white wine with buttered almonds: Energy 347kcal/1453kJ; Protein 34.1g; Carbohydrate 2.4g, of which sugars 1.8g; Fat 17.2g, of which saturates 4.2g; Cholesterol 111mg; Calcium 68mg; Fibre 1.1g; Sodium 113mg.

Trout with cucumber cream: Energy 398kcal/1663kJ; Protein 41.1g; Carbohydrate 3.7g, of which sugars 3.2g; Fat 22.9g, of which saturates 10g; Cholesterol 168mg; Calcium 95mg; Fibre 0.8g; Sodium 150mg.

Thai-style trout: Energy 174kcal/735kJ; Protein 23g; Carbohydrate 7g, of which sugars 6g; Fat 6g, of which saturates 1g; Cholesterol 77mg; Calcium 48mg; Fibre 0g; Sodium 230mg.

Trout with crunchy peppercorns: Energy 349kcal/1459kJ; Protein 40g; Carbohydrate 0g, of which sugars 0g; Fat 21.6g, of which saturates 3.8g; Cholesterol 134mg; Calcium 68mg; Fibre 0g; Sodium 93mg.

Stuffed trout with tarragon sauce: Energy 487kcal/2033kJ; Protein 29g; Carbohydrate 26g, of which sugars 26g; Fat 30g, of which saturates 5g; Cholesterol 84mg; Calcium 106mg; Fibre 2g; Sodium 313mg.

Trout fillets in a creamy mustard sauce: Energy 570kcal/2387kJ; Protein 47.9g; Carbohydrate 42.5g, of which sugars 5.1g; Fat 24.1g, of which saturates 6.9g; Cholesterol 126mg; Calcium 62mg; Fibre 2.7g; Sodium 738mg

Whole glazed trout with cucumber salad: Energy 375kcal/1580kJ; Protein 59.1g; Carbohydrate 9.3g, of which sugars 9.2g; Fat 11.5g, of which saturates 2.6g; Cholesterol 240mg; Calcium 133mg; Fibre 1.1g; Sodium 224mg.

Poached trout with fennel: Energy 461kcal/1937kJ; Protein 38.8g; Carbohydrate 31.4g, of which sugars 5.4g; Fat 17.7g, of which saturates 8.5g; Cholesterol 173mg; Calcium 90mg; Fibre 3.9g; Sodium 259mg.

Garlic baked trout with avocado salad: Energy 178kcal/744kJ; Protein 13g; Carbohydrate 6g, of which sugars 5g; Fat 11g, of which saturates 2g; Cholesterol 40mg; Calcium 39mg; Fibre 2g; Sodium 125mg.

Stuffed trout with orange sauce: Energy 333kcal/1395kJ; Protein 31g; Carbohydrate 13.8g, of which sugars 8.2g; Fat 17.5g, of which saturates 8.2g; Cholesterol 196mg; Calcium 89mg; Fibre 1.8g; Sodium 253mg.

Trout with prosciutto: Energy 369kcal/1546kJ; Protein 48g; Carbohydrate 0.6g, of which sugars 0.6g; Fat 19.4g, of which saturates 8.8g; Cholesterol 216mg; Calcium 66mg; Fibre 0g; Sodium 821mg.

Rainbow trout in lemon and mustard marinade: Energy 368.8kcal/1542kJ; Protein 40.7g; Carbohydrate 9.1g, of which sugars 5.9g; Fat 19.2g, of which saturates 3g; Cholesterol 160mg; Calcium 114.5mg; Fibre 2g; Sodium 153mg.

Baked trout with caraway: Energy 478kcal/2009kj; Protein 42g; Carbohydrate 36g of which sugars 2g; Fat 20g, of which saturates 2g; Cholesterol 0mg; Calcium 49mg; Fibre 2.4g; Sodium 622mg.

Trout with orange and herbs: Energy 459kcal/1922kJ; Protein 41g; Carbohydrate 17g, of which sugars 17g; Fat 26g, of which saturates 4g; Cholesterol 134mg; Calcium 130mg; Fibre 4g; Sodium 100mg.

Baked trout with cream sauce: Energy 640kcal/2653kj; Protein 40g; Carbohydrate 4g, of which sugars 1g; Fat 51g, of which saturates 27g; Cholesterol 112mg; Calcium 56mg; Fibre 0.1g; Sodium 300mg.

Trout with leek and bacon: Energy 324kcal/1357kJ; Protein 44.4g; Carbohydrate 0.4g, of which sugars 0.3g; Fat 16.1g, of which saturates 5.1g; Cholesterol 174mg; Calcium 60mg; Fibre 0.3g; Sodium 997mg

Liquorice, walnut and fennel trout fillets: Energy 333kcal/1395kJ; Protein 31g; Carbohydrate 13.8g, of which sugars 8.2g; Fat 17.5g, of which saturates 8.2g; Cholesterol 196mg; Calcium 89mg; Fibre 1.8g; Sodium 253mg.

Baked trout with tomato sauce: Energy 420kcal/1751kJ; Protein 30g; Carbohydrate 3g, of which sugars 3g; Fat 23g, of which saturates 4g; Cholesterol 101mg; Calcium 56mg; Fibre 0.7g; Sodium 103mg.

Fried trout with Chinese wine sauce: Energy 300kcal/1251kJ; Protein 22g; Carbohydrate 6g, of which sugars 2g; Fat 20g,
of which saturates 3g; Cholesterol 75mg; Calcium 30mg; Fibre 1g; Sodium 546mg.

Trout fried in flour: Energy 699kcal/2935kJ; Protein 55.1g; Carbohydrate 52.7g, of which sugars 10g; Fat 31.3g, of which saturates 16.3g; Cholesterol 250mg; Calcium 221mg; Fibre 3.9g; Sodium 438mg.

Trout gougère: Energy 450kcal/1872kJ; Protein 25.9g; Carbohydrate 18.1g, of which sugars 3.5g; Fat 28.3g, of which saturates 12.8g; Cholesterol 97mg; Calcium 242mg; Fibre 1.3g; Sodium 320mg.

Trout and asparagus pie: Energy 310kcal/1293kJ; Protein 17g; Carbohydrate 13g, of which sugars 3g; Fat 21g, of which saturates 12g; Cholesterol 87mg; Calcium 109mg; Fibre 1g; Sodium 236mg.

Trout with black rice: Energy 590kcal/2468kJ; Protein 50.9g; Carbohydrate 62.4g, of which sugars 2.3g; Fat 14.8g, of which saturates 0.9g; Cholesterol 0mg; Calcium 55mg; Fibre 1.2g; Sodium 1198mg.

Smoked trout risotto: Energy 641kcal/2676kJ; Protein 34.9g; Carbohydrate 83.6g, of which sugars 2.8g; Fat 18.1g, of which saturates 6.7g; Cholesterol 54mg; Calcium 197mg; Fibre 1.7g; Sodium 1739mg.

Spicy trout risotto: Energy 615kcal/2565kJ; Protein 29.9g; Carbohydrate 70.1g, of which sugars 0.3g; Fat 20.3g, of which saturates 11.2g; Cholesterol 139mg; Calcium 59mg; Fibre 0g; Sodium 229mg.

Trout and prosciutto rolls: Energy 397kcal/1662kJ; Protein 33g; Carbohydrate 43.6g, of which sugars 1.1g; Fat 7.6g, of which saturates 0.3g; Cholesterol 29mg; Calcium 37mg; Fibre 0.2g; Sodium 202mg.

Trout with rice, tomatoes and nuts: Energy 501kcal/2094kJ; Protein 46g; Carbohydrate 27.8g, of which sugars 5g; Fat 22.8g, of which saturates 3.3g; Cholesterol 160mg; Calcium 144mg; Fibre 3.2g; Sodium 161mg.

Quinoa-stuffed trout: Energy 478kcal/2008kJ; Protein 37g; Carbohydrate 45g, of which sugars 18g; Fat 18g, of which saturates 3g; Cholesterol 98mg; Calcium 97mg; Fibre 7g; Sodium 494mg

Malaysian steamed trout with noodles: Energy 774kcal/3525kJ; Protein 56g; Carbohydrate 64g, of which sugars 3g; Fat 34g, of which saturates 12g; Cholesterol 180mg; Calcium 72mg; Fibre 4g; Sodium 265mg.

Fusilli with smoked trout: Energy 410kcal/1735kJ; Protein 23.4g; Carbohydrate 62.3g, of which sugars 12g; Fat 9.3g, of which saturates 2.1g; Cholesterol 21mg; Calcium 186mg; Fibre 4.5g; Sodium 919mg.

Spicy trout cannelloni: Energy 410kcal/1735kJ; Protein 23.4g; Carbohydrate 62.3g, of which sugars 12g; Fat 9.3g, of which saturates 2.1g; Cholesterol 21mg; Calcium 186mg; Fibre 4.5g; Sodium 919mg.

Smoked trout pasta salad: Energy 369kcal/1548kJ; Protein 14.5g; Carbohydrate 42.7g, of which sugars 2.8g; Fat 16.8g, of which saturates 4g; Cholesterol 29mg; Calcium 31mg; Fibre 2.3g; Sodium 613mg.

Trout burgers: Energy 461kcal/1936kJ; Protein 18g; Carbohydrate 47g, of which sugars 6g; Fat 23g, of which saturates 4g; Cholesterol 72mg; Calcium 120mg; Fibre 4g; Sodium 484mg.

Cheese-topped trout: Energy 524kcal/2185kJ; Protein 51.3g; Carbohydrate 10.3g, of which sugars 0.9g; Fat 31.1g, of which saturates 8.9g; Cholesterol 34mg; Calcium 214mg; Fibre 1g; Sodium 422mg.

Hot and fragrant trout: Energy 267kcal/1125kJ; Protein 36g; Carbohydrate 11g, of which sugars 8g; Fat 9g, of which saturates 2g; Cholesterol 117mg; Calcium 54mg; Fibre 1g; Sodium 394mg.

Trout in wine sauce with barbecued plantain: Energy 478kcal/2005kJ; Protein 36g; Carbohydrate 30g, of which sugars 8g; Fat 8g, of which saturates 25g; Cholesterol 131mg; Calcium 52mg; Fibre 2g; Sodium 679mg.

Spicy barbecued sea trout: Energy 174kcal/735kJ; Protein 23g; Carbohydrate 7g, of which sugars 6g; Fat.39g, of which saturates 1g; Cholesterol 77mg; Calcium 48mg; Fibre 0g; Sodium 590mg.

Baon-wrapped trout with oatmeal: Energy 997kcal/4164kJ; Protein 85g; Carbohydrate 25g, of which sugars 3g; Fat 63g, of which saturates 19g; Cholesterol 326mg; Calcium 118mg; Fibre 3g; Sodium 1190mg.

Stuffed grilled trout: Energy 661kcal/2761kJ; Protein 40.9g; Carbohydrate 34.9g, of which sugars 1.2g; Fat 40.7g, of which saturates 6.2g; Cholesterol 147mg; Calcium 114mg; Fibre 1g; Sodium 475mg.

Trout with curried orange butter: Energy 354kcal/1481kJ; Protein 44g; Carbohydrate 0g, of which sugars 0g; Fat 20g, of which saturates 6g; Cholesterol 164mg; Calcium 45mg; Fibre 0g; Sodium 141mg.

Index